85 Engaging Movement Activities

Related Resources from High/Scope Press

Movement and Music Materials

Teaching Movement & Dance: A Sequential Approach to Rhythmic Movement, Fourth Ed.
Round the Circle: Key Experiences in Movement for Children
Movement Plus Music: Activities for Children Ages 3 to 7, Second Ed.
Movement Plus Rhymes, Songs, & Singing Games
Movement in Steady Beat
Rhythmically Moving 1–9 (cassettes, CDs)
Changing Directions 1–5 (cassettes, CDs)
Rhythmically Walking (cassettes)

Elementary Curriculum Guides

Foundations in Elementary Education: Movement
Foundations in Elementary Education: Music
Foundations in Elementary Education: Overview
Language & Literacy
Mathematics
Science

Elementary Activity Books

Literature-Based Workshops for Language Arts—Ideas for Active Learning Grades K–2
Literature-Based Workshops for Mathematics—Ideas for Active Learning Grades K–2
Life and Environment: Elementary Science Activity Series
Structure and Form: Elementary Science Activity Series
Energy and Change: Elementary Science Activity Series

Elementary Curriculum Videotapes

Active Learning
Classroom Environment
Language & Literacy
Mathematics

Available from
HIGH/SCOPE® PRESS
A division of the High/Scope Educational Research Foundation
600 North River Street
Ypsilanti, MI 48198-2898
734/485-2000, FAX 734/485-0704
E-mail: press@highscope.org   Web site: www.highscope.org

LEARNING ON THE MOVE
K-6

85 Engaging Movement Activities

Phyllis S. Weikart

Elizabeth B. Carlton

HIGH/SCOPE® PRESS

Ypsilanti, Michigan

Published by

HIGH/SCOPE® PRESS

A division of the HIGH/SCOPE EDUCATIONAL RESEARCH FOUNDATION

600 NORTH RIVER STREET

YPSILANTI, MICHIGAN 48198-2898

734/485-2000, FAX 734/485-0704

press@highscope.org

Editor: Nancy Brickman

Cover design, text design: Margaret FitzGerald, Metaphor Marketing Inc.

Photography: Gregory Fox Photography

Library of Congress Cataloging-in-Publication Data

Weikart, Phyllis S., 1931-
  85 engaging movement activities / Phyllis S. Weikart, Elizabeth B.
Carlton.
        p. cm.
  Includes index.
   ISBN 1-57379-125-3 (softcover : alk. paper)
   1. Movement education. 2. Active learning. 3. Education,
Elementary--Activity programs. I. Title: Eighty-five engaging movement
activities. II. Carlton, Elizabeth B. III. Title.
   GV452 .W42 2002
   372.86'8--dc21

                         2002007489

ISBN 1-57379-125-3

Printed in the United States of America

10 9 8 7 6 5 4 3 2 1

Contents

Preface ix

A Movement-Based Active Learning Process 1

Introduction to the Activities 11

Kindergarten and Above
1. Creativity With Scarves 16
2. Explore That Sound 18
3. Low or High 20
4. Musical Houses 22
5. Names in Beat 24
6. Stop Sign 26
7. Traveling Pathways Between Objects 28
8. Attributes of Shapes 30
9. Listening and Identifying 32
10. Lively Levels 34
11. Planning to Step 36
12. Seven Jumps 38
13. People in Our Town 40
14. Understanding Spatial Concepts 42
15. Who's Driving? 44
16. Simon Says Variation 46
17. We Keep the Beat Together 48

Grade 1 and Above
18. Is the Pattern Even or Uneven? 52
19. Statue Clones 54
20. Matching Stick-Figure Poses 56
21. Action Words 58
22. Different Shape—Different Movement 60
23. Combining Words 62
24. Statues That Change 64

25. Beat Echo 66
26. Echo Sequence 68
27. Extending Our Movements 70
28. Making Pathways in the Air 72
29. Is It Macrobeat or Microbeat? 74
30. Puppets 76
31. Pushing Up 78
32. Recalling the Past 80
33. Stop and Balance 82
34. Trains 84
35. Traveling Pathways Without Objects 86
36. Who Matches Me? 88
37. Numbers and Statue Shapes 90
38. How Many Points of Contact? 92
39. Beat-Keeping With Mallets 94
40. Creating Designs 96
41. Creative Paper Plates 98
42. Estimating Distance and Time 100
43. Spelling Song 102

Grade 2 and Above

44. From Back to Front 106
45. Hearing and Responding 108
46. Mirroring 110
47. Moves to Remember 112
48. Moving to a Rhyme 114
49. Plate Dancing 116
50. Passing Game Lead-Up 118
51. Plate Aerobics 120
52. Robots 122
53. Same and Different 124
54. Sounds 126
55. What Else Do You See? 128

Grade 3 and Above

56. Flipping Sticks 132
57. Greater or Lesser Numbers 134
58. Human Clock 136
59. Matching Statues 138
60. The Sum Moves Like This 140

61. Aerobic Integration 142

62. Combining Beat and Rhythm 144

63. Combining Sequences 146

64. Echo Canon 148

65. Hand-Jives 150

66. Hand-to-Hand Passing 152

67. Integrated Movement Copycat 154

68. Integrated Sequences 156

69. The Moving Circle 158

70. Reverse That Image 160

71. What Beat Shall We Use? 162

72. Adding Arms to the Dance 164

73. Conducting and Walking 166

74. Grand March 168

75. Identifying Angles 170

76. Machines That Work 172

77. Shaping Sequences 174

78. Is the Movement Straight or Circular? 176

79. Synonyms and Antonyms 178

80. And Three It Will Be 180

81. Timing Relationships 182

82. Strengthening Math Facts 184

83. Forward and Backward 186

84. Combining Groups of Two and Three 188

85. Categories of Nouns 190

Glossary 193

Alphabetical Index to the Activities 199

Musical Selections Provided With This Book 203

Preface

This idea book is written as an activity supplement to *Teaching Movement & Dance: A Sequential Approach to Rhythmic Movement* by Phyllis S. Weikart. It is the first book in the *Learning on the Move* series to be developed by the Movement and Music Education Division of the High/Scope Educational Research Foundation. Many of these activities were originally part of *Foundations in Elementary Education: Movement* by Phyllis S. Weikart and Elizabeth B. Carlton. The activities from *Foundations* have been revised, and new activities have been added.

    The movement activities are drawn from our personal experiences with students in the elementary grades as well as experiences shared by trainers in High/Scope's **"Education Through Movement: Building the Foundation"** program. We are sharing these active learning experiences with you because it is our belief that purposeful movement (movement that is planned, executed, and reflected upon) can help curriculum concepts come to life. Our work over the years has had an academic emphasis; we have tried to help students become engaged and excited not only about using their movement abilities but also about the entire educational process.

    The activities in this book are organized into four categories: kindergarten and above, grade 1 and above, grade 2 and above, and grade 3 and above. The designation "and older" indicates that most activities can be used across the elementary grades if the age of the learner is taken into consideration and the method of presentation is adjusted for that age. Each activity includes extensions that may be used to tailor the activity for older and younger learners, a list of key experiences in movement and music that pertain to the activity, and, when applicable, suggestions for recorded music from High/Scope's *Rhythmically Moving* (RM) or *Changing Directions* (CD) series. (Many of these selections are included in the CD provided with this book.) The music is referenced in the materials list.

Please be certain to read the opening two chapters before trying the activities. The first chapter contains important information on how to engage learners in experiences using the **movement-based active learning process.** Active learning is a hallmark of the High/Scope Foundation's work. The addition of "movement-based" brings a movement focus to this learning process. The second chapter explains how each activity is organized.

We would like to extend grateful appreciation and heartfelt thanks to our families, to the individuals in the "Education Through Movement" network who have been so supportive and helpful, to our editor, Nancy Brickman, and to our graphic designer, Margaret FitzGerald. We would also like to acknowledge Karen Sawyers, Assistant Director of High/Scope's Movement and Music Education Division, who has been very helpful throughout this effort.

We hope you will find this idea book to be a useful addition to your movement and music materials for elementary-aged students. Eighty additional music activities that also use movement as a base are found in *Foundations in Elementary Education: Music* by Elizabeth B. Carlton and Phyllis Weikart. These activities use the music key experiences to strengthen all aspects of learners' musical foundation from kindergarten to grade 3.

A Movement-Based Active Learning Process

The "Education Through Movement: Building the Foundation" program includes an approach to teaching and learning that stresses process as well as content. In this learning process, *learners and teachers are partners*—mutual initiators and supporters of learning. In the pages that follow, we discuss each of the four components of the **movement-based active learning process:**

- **Key experiences** in movement and music
- **Movement core**
- **Teaching Model**
- **Active learning support strategies**

This is the "delivery system" that teachers keep in mind as they facilitate students' learning.

The Key Experiences in Movement and Music

The **key experiences in movement and music** are one of the components of the **movement-based active learning process.** The complete list and detailed information about **key experiences in music** are found in *Foundations in Elementary Education: Music* by Elizabeth B. Carlton & Phyllis S. Weikart. Only those music key experiences that are essential for each activity are listed with the activity; these music key experiences highlight important connections between music and movement. The nine **key experiences in movement** for elementary-aged students described in this activity book provide the framework for the **movement-based active learning process.** These experiences all involve **purposeful movement,** in which an intent is expressed through decision making, planning, doing, recalling, or imitating. We use these key experiences to recognize, support, and extend the learner's fundamental abilities in order to achieve success and understanding in movement, music, and in other curriculum areas.

The **movement key experiences** referred to in this book are as follows:

✓ *Acting upon movement directions*

✓ *Describing movement*

✓ *Moving in nonlocomotor ways*

✓ *Moving in locomotor ways*

✓ *Moving in integrated ways*

✓ *Moving with objects*

✓ *Expressing creativity in movement*

✓ *Feeling and expressing steady beat*

✓ *Moving in sequences to a common beat*

Taken together, these nine key experiences are designed for learners of any age, except for *moving in integrated ways,* which is appropriate only for second grade and above.

These movement key experiences build a strong foundation for learning, because they encompass a broad range of kinesthetic experiences that students need to function effectively, both academically and in the arts. In addition to strength, balance, and timing, these experiences help children develop steady beat independence; the ability to attend, focus, and concentrate; physical coordination; creativity; language skills; problem solving; planning; and decision making.

By keeping the nine movement key experiences in mind, teachers can go beyond just conveying information. The key experiences help teachers focus on students' learning processes: Are students attending to what is said? Do students understand what they are hearing, seeing, or feeling? What about creativity and problem solving? Is each student competent with steady beat and with sequences of movement in steady beat? How can we encourage students to lead one another, to share their ideas, and to follow another's movement suggestions?

Associated with each key experience in movement or music are specific **learning objectives** that permit teachers to assess students' progress in physical, cognitive, social, and artistic areas. Each key experience and its intended objectives are listed opposite.

Movement Core

Having looked briefly at the first component of the **movement-based active learning process,** we now examine the **movement core.** This second component assists learners

Key Experience	Learning Objectives
Acting upon movement directions	Seeing and perceiving; hearing and comprehending; feeling and identifying
Describing movement	Using thinking and language abilities (moving and describing; planning; recalling; linking movement with a word—SAY & DO)
Moving in nonlocomotor ways	Achieving comfort and awareness of anchored movement in personal space
Moving in locomotor ways	Achieving comfort and awareness of nonanchored movement in personal and general space
Moving in integrated ways	Achieving comfort with and (grade 2 and up) awareness of nonlocomotor and locomotor movement purposefully combined
Moving with objects	Achieving comfort with and awareness of nonlocomotor, locomotor, and integrated movement when using objects
Expressing creativity in movement	Extending movement by using one's own ideas
Feeling and expressing steady beat	Independently expressing and maintaining steady beat to rhymes, songs, and recorded or live music
Moving in sequences to a common beat	Sequencing movement alone and with others

to experience success with the key experiences in movement and music.

The **movement core,** illustrated in the diagrams on page 4, is a summary of the motor-development base of purposeful movement for all ages in the High/Scope "Education Through Movement: Building the Foundation" program. Note that one of the **movement core** diagrams is labeled "nonlocomotor" and the other, "locomotor." In each diagram, the text inside the circle refers to the way the body can be organized for purposeful movement.

Each diagram illustrates the progression of movement complexity from the top to the bottom of the circle—with the easiest movements at the top and the most complex at the bottom. As teachers introduce movement to students of any age, these progressions from simple to complex should be kept in mind. As the diagram indicates, "two sides" is the easiest pattern when using nonlocomotor movement, movement of the upper body, e.g., patting, shaking, swinging, or bending/straightening. "Alternating sides" is the easiest pattern when using locomotor movement, e.g., marching, walking, jogging. "One side...other side" refers to movements repeated on one side of the body and then on the other side. For nonlocomotor movement, movements are easiest to follow when both sides of the body are moving symmetrically. Moving one side in repetition followed by

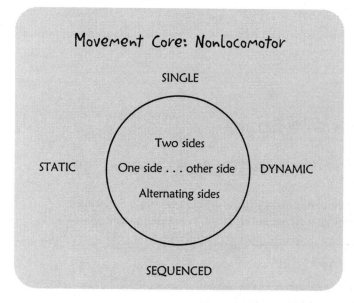

Movement Core: Nonlocomotor

SINGLE

STATIC   Two sides   DYNAMIC
        One side . . . other side
           Alternating sides

SEQUENCED

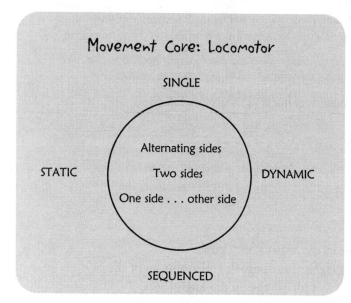

Movement Core: Locomotor

SINGLE

STATIC   Alternating sides   DYNAMIC
           Two sides
        One side . . . other side

SEQUENCED

the other side is more difficult, and alternating sides is the most difficult of these movement patterns. For locomotor movement, alternating sides is the easiest pattern, followed by two sides (e.g., jumping), followed by one side in repetition (e.g., hopping).

The words placed around the circle of each **movement core** diagram refer to the ways that the body executes purposeful movement.

"Single" movements, are those that can be labeled with one word spoken over and over, e.g., "march, march, march, march" or "pound, pound, pound, pound."

"Sequenced" movements, have two or more labels, e.g., "bend, straighten; bend, straighten" or "head, shoulders; knees shoulders."

"Single" movements are easier than **"sequenced"** movements.

"Static" movements are those that pause in the desired location before another movement starts.

"Dynamic" movements keep on going. **"Static"** movements are easier than **"dynamic"** ones.

Teaching Model

The ease with which students, young people, and adults grasp movement demonstrations or directions often depends on whether the teacher's verbal directions or demonstrations are based on the **Teaching Model** and **movement core.**

The three-part **Teaching Model** described here was developed as part of the "Education Through Movement" program. However, it can be applied to any subject area. Educators in math, science, reading, music, physical education, dance, special education, and drama report using the model successfully. They have found the model's three components—**separate, simplify,** and **facilitate**—can lead to increased success, to a sense of responsibility in learners, and to a decreased need to reteach concepts after they have been introduced. A close look at each of the components may explain why such favorable results occur.

The "Separate" Component

This component involves initiating experiences or presenting information by using *only one mode of presentation* at a time. By "mode of presentation" we are referring to three distinct ways that teachers may present material. Each mode corresponds to a different kind of sensory information that students process, as follows:

- **Demonstration,** which students must visually process in order to respond
- **Verbal (spoken or sung) directions,** which students must *aurally* process in order to respond
- **Hands-on (tactile) guidance,** which students must process *by interpreting the "felt" movement* in order to respond

By choosing to **separate,** that is, by using only one of these three modes of presentation at a time, the teacher enables students to focus on a single message. Combining two or more modes of presentation—telling while showing, or telling while giving hands-on guidance, for example—usually gives students too much sensory input. Instead of integrating the input from different senses, some students tend to respond to such dual messages by relying on their strongest learning modality. As a result, they may block out information from the other senses, or worse yet, they miss the information entirely because of the confusion of using two senses at once. However, it is important to maintain an appropriate balance between the different modes of presentation. To do so, teachers must consider what each mode involves:

Demonstration. The teacher usually precedes the demonstration with a statement that gains everyone's attention and lets them know a demonstration will follow. ("Watch what my arms do, and join me when you are ready.") The teacher then demonstrates *without speaking.* Many tasks are effectively demonstrated with this silent method. When it is necessary for a movement to be done in a specific way, this technique is often more effective then using verbal directions.

Verbal (spoken or sung) directions. The teacher usually precedes the verbal presentation with a statement like "Please listen and follow these directions." This lets everyone know that important directions are going to follow. *Without demonstrating,* the teacher then **tells** students what to do. ("Find as many different ways as you can to travel in a straight pathway.") Teachers have found that using only verbal directions often works well when the movement does not need to be performed in an exact way. Hearing a description allows students to interpret and respond to the directions in individual ways.

Hands-on guidance. The teacher, after gaining permission to touch the student, might say, "I'm going to raise your arms over your head." Then, *without further speaking,* the teacher uses hands-on guidance to raise the student's arms. Thus, the verbal prompt and hands-on guidance do not occur at the same time.

The "Simplify" Component

This component involves beginning with what is easy or manageable to process, so all students can become immediately engaged and experience success. To **simplify,** the teacher first considers students' present capabilities. The teacher also determines the subtasks that make up the task, using knowledge of prerequisite skills. Taking these factors into account, the teacher determines which subtasks are appropriate to the level of the class and begins there.

Observing students when they are exploring movement or when they are working with partners or in small groups can aid teachers in selecting and promoting active learning experiences that are appropriate to students' needs, interests, and levels. Occasionally, teachers express concern that using the **simplify** strategy slows them down. Our reply is that using this component is well worth the extra few minutes required, if it results in students attaining true ownership of concepts.

Following are some guidelines for the **simplify** strategy. They are summarized on the chart on the next page.

The "Facilitate" Component

The first two components of the Teaching Model, **separate** and **simplify,** are strategies that teachers use in presenting concepts and in planning and initiating activities. The third and last component of the Teaching Model—the **facilitate** strategy—concerns the ways teachers engage students through action, thought, and language to support them in constructing their own knowledge.

Teachers **facilitate** when they encourage and support students in initiating their own ideas and experiences. They **facilitate** when they give students time to explore concepts on their own, to apply existing knowledge to a task. They **facilitate** when they give students time to explore movement concepts with partners or in small groups, planning and making choices about how they will solve problems.

Guidelines for Simplifying Movement

Simple ⟶	More Complex ⟶	Most Complex
static movement		dynamic movement
movement with endpoints against body		movement with endpoints away from body
upper-body movement		weight-bearing lower-body movements
trunk movement	limb movement	finger, toe movement
gross-motor movement		fine-motor movement
nonlocomotor movement	locomotor movement	integrated nonlocomotor and locomotor movement
movement without object		movement with object
symmetrical movements		asymmetrical movements
nonlocomotor: two sides	one side	alternating sides
locomotor: alternating sides	two sides	one side
single movement		sequenced movement
personal space		general space
movement alone with one's internal beat		movement alone with specified external beat
movement alone with one's internal beat		movement timed with a partner or group
nonlocomotor movement to a slower beat		nonlocomotor movement to a faster beat
locomotor movement to a beat close to one's internal beat		locomotor movement to a beat unlike one's internal beat
right and left not specified		right and left specified

Teachers also **facilitate** when they encourage descriptive language from students and when they listen and respond to the language students use among themselves. Asking students to talk about what they are going to do (planning) to describe their current actions (doing), and to reflect on what they did (recalling) are other ways to **facilitate.** Finally, providing a safe, interactive environment where teachers and students work as partners and support one another is the most important of the ways that teachers **facilitate** the learning process.

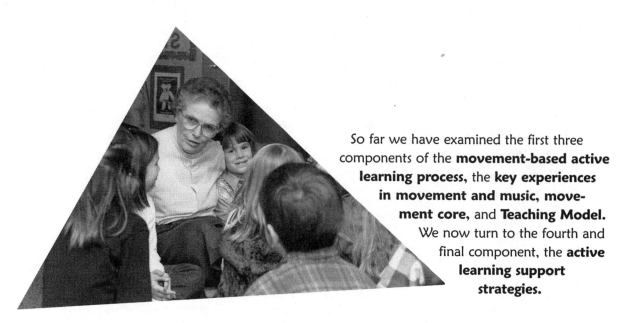

So far we have examined the first three components of the **movement-based active learning process,** the **key experiences in movement and music, movement core,** and **Teaching Model.** We now turn to the fourth and final component, the **active learning support strategies.**

Active Learning Support Strategies

Dictionary definitions of "teach" often include phrases like "to impart knowledge or skills," to "show or help to learn." Of these phrases, the most significant to us is "help to learn." These words describe the teacher's **facilitative role** and suggest the **teacher/ learner partnership** that is central to *education through movement.* We believe the teacher's role is not to be a director of students' activities and a dispenser of information. "Teaching does not imply learning." Instead, in keeping with the High/Scope philosophy, an **active learning approach** is used. Our goal is to transform students from passive receivers of information to active constructors of their own knowledge. When teaching is approached in this way, students become absorbed in their learning tasks and usually display an energy and zeal that are often lacking in teacher-directed classrooms.

In this approach, the teacher both introduces ideas and recognizes opportunities—the "teachable moments" when ideas initiated by students may be supported and extended. Because "to do is to understand," this initiation of ideas by both teacher and students is supported across the curriculum. Students plan variations on basic movements, make choices, share ideas, and talk about their experiences to promote greater awareness of curriculum concepts.

The following are basic strategies of the **active learning approach** as developed in the "Education Through Movement" program:

- **Initiation by teacher and students** is critical to successful learning. When student ideas are incorporated in the experience, teachers find that students generally maintain high interest. Furthermore, the ideas that are mutually generated far surpass those generated by teachers alone.

- **Exploration of purposeful movement** leads to true understanding and the ability to apply curriculum concepts. This kind of exploration involves thought and intention rather than random activity.

- **Choices and planning by students** enable them to be actively involved in the learning process. Students take on ownership of the task and its solutions.

- **Language listened to and supplied** implies much verbal interaction as students verbally describe and suggest movements and listen to others do so. Conversations occur among students and between the teacher and students. An important teacher strategy is to reinforce with language many of the things students are doing. This assists students in developing cognitive understanding. By supplying language, teachers also help students *transfer learning* to make associations from existing knowledge to new knowledge.

- **Reflection** encourages students to learn by thinking back on their experiences. Students are encouraged to reflect on their experiences, to draw

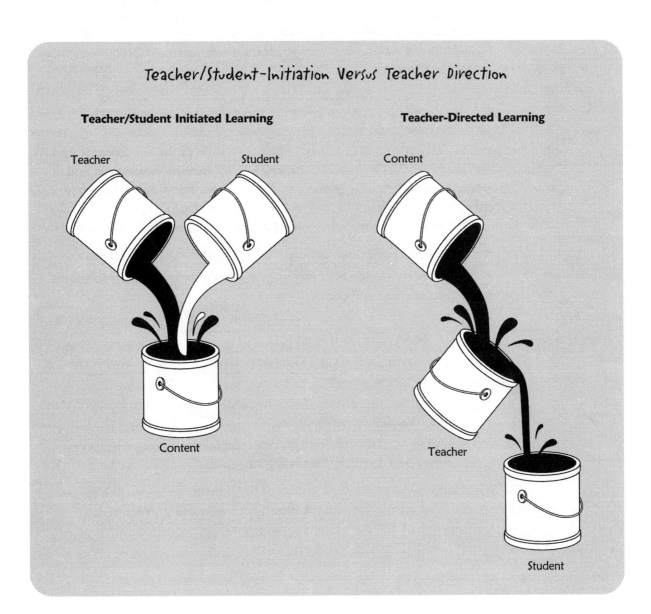

Teacher/Student-Initiation Versus Teacher Direction

Teacher/Student Initiated Learning

Teacher   Student

Content

Teacher-Directed Learning

Content

Teacher

Student

conclusions, to think about other ways they might have proceeded, and to think of what made the experience easy or difficult. This kind of reflection helps teachers determine if further experiences are necessary to achieve ownership of a particular concept.

- **Support from teachers and peers** implies the creation of a supportive environment in which students feel they have a say in their own learning. Providing a positive, supportive classroom atmosphere means realizing that teachers and students are on the educational journey together; each person brings something valid to this journey. Students who try and still fall short of the "correct" answer are *on the way to getting it right*; no one who tries is ever completely wrong. If teachers set this positive tone in the classroom, students will support one another, and the classroom will become an exciting place to learn.

Summary

In this chapter, we have described four very important aspects of the environment for *education through movement*. Taken together, the **key experiences in movement and music, movement core, Teaching Model,** and **active learning support strategies** constitute a method teachers can use to inspire or "lead from behind." The signs of this kind of leadership are obvious to anyone observing students. In such an environment, students

- Explore ideas rather than passively accept what the teacher dictates
- Have opportunities to lead and make choices instead of always following the teacher's lead and choices
- Feel free to express ideas instead of thinking that they can only speak when asked a question by the teacher
- Feel safe in trying out ideas and making mistakes instead of always needing to have the "right" answer
- Are encouraged by positive, descriptive statements from the teacher instead of by individual, judgmental praise
- Respond to teacher's comforting voice-tone instead of responding only when they hear forceful, threatening language

The next chapter presents the organization of the activities to follow. It is followed by the 85 activities that use the **movement-based active learning process.**

Introduction to the Activities

The 85 activities contained in this book provide teachers and parents with ideas for guiding students' understanding and for helping them develop ownership of the skills and concepts implicit in the High/Scope **movement and music key experiences** and the elementary curriculum. As you use the suggestions these activities contain for teacher-initiated active learning experiences, watch for opportunities to support student-initiated learning as well. We hope our suggestions will give you a way to begin to work within the framework of the **movement-based active learning process.** For ease of use, the activities are numbered throughout this book. (An alphabetical index to the activities appears on page 199.)

Before attempting the activities, we recommend reading the preceding chapter, which describes the four components of the **movement-based active learning process: the key experiences, movement core, Teaching Model,** and **active learning support strategies.** We hope these activities will become a part of the total educational approach used in your classroom, gym, music room, or home.

Activity Elements

Each activity contains the following elements:

- **Grade level:** The earliest grade suggested for the activity is stated. However, each activity and/or extension of the activity may be presented to older and younger students as well, provided that age-appropriate strategies are used to adapt the experiences to children's levels.

- **Movement and music key experiences:** The movement and music key experiences you might observe for students' growth are listed at the top of the activity.

- **Possible curriculum concepts:** Curriculum concepts listed may include knowledge and skills in movement, physical education, music, and other academic and nonacademic areas. As you plan your activity, choose the concepts that best match your reasons for initiating the activity.

- **Description:** A brief description of the activity is given in large type.

- **Materials:** Materials to be used in the activity are listed next, including selections from recordings in the *Rhythmically Moving* (RM) and *Changing Directions* (CD) series from High/Scope Press. Selections that are also included on the CD provided with this book are listed first. (Additional activity ideas for music selections on *Rhythmically Moving 1–5* may be found in *Guide to Rhythmically Moving 1–5* by Elizabeth B. Carlton and Phyllis S. Weikart.)

- **Activity to experience:** Suggested steps to follow in presenting the activity are described in this section. You may wish to omit some steps or to include others not listed, depending on the environment and ability levels of your students. We urge you to include the exploration phase of the activity when suggested.

- **Facilitation and reflection:** This section contains sample questions you may pose. The specific questions you use, of course, will depend on the age

and experience of your students. You do not need to ask all of them. These questions are included because it is our philosophy that *thought* and *language* must be added to action to help students reach true ownership of movement, music, and curriculum concepts.

- **Extensions:** These are suggested ways to expand, modify, or simplify the activity to make it applicable for older or younger students. There are also suggestions for extending the activity into other curriculum areas.

Ten Hints For Success

Practical guidelines for implementing the activities:

1. **Devise ways for students to be as inconspicuous as possible.** Many learners, particularly older learners, prefer to first try new movements while they are seated, if this is possible. For all types of movement activities, have students stand in a loose formation rather than a formal circle. A loose formation provides a "safety net."

2. **Initiate movement without reference to specific sides of the body (right or left).** If a particular movement involves using or beginning with only one side of the body, refer to it as "one side" or "your favorite" side. Then refer to the "other" side, because it is important to try movement on both sides. Alternating movements can begin with either side.

3. **Try to avoid posing movement problems that have a definite "right" or "wrong" solution.** Students' initial exploration should involve doing a movement in the way they choose to do it. Correctness should not be required until students have had a chance for trial-and-error experimentation.

4. **Introduce movement experiences in personal space before using general space (when possible).** Many locomotor movements, such as stepping, jumping and hopping, can be performed in *personal space* before they are done in *general space*.* This gives students a chance to develop the balance and coordination required for the movement.

5. **Save partner work and small-group work for later.** Many students are uncomfortable with purposeful movement at first. Having a partner or working in a small group is intimidating until they have had a chance to explore a movement on their own. Whether you use this suggestion depends on the students you work with. You may find they are comfortable working with others, in which case they may not need this approach. You know your students.

6. **Use movement and creative representation experiences that are age-appropriate.** Patting parts of the body such as the head, chin, or ears is appropriate for younger children but may seem "babyish" to older learners. However, if the suggestion to pat the head comes from a student, then it works even with "cool" fifth graders. Younger students delight in moving in ways that represent events or animals, but older learners usually do not.

Personal space refers to all the space that a person remains in while stepping or jumping or can reach while the body is anchored in place, as opposed to general space, which includes all the space available where the activity is taking place, in an area of a room or within the boundaries of an outdoor space.

7. **Begin creative movement experiences by giving hints to aid in problem solving.** For example, it may help students if the following is said, "If you need an idea in order to begin, look around at what others are doing and copy first."

8. **Give students time to "try a movement on for size" before asking them to do it together with others, to a common beat.** Students need to move to their own internal timing to develop comfort with a movement before they synchronize the movement with other students.

9. **Introduce action songs and similar active learning experiences by presenting the movement first.** Once students are successful with the movement, then add on the rhyme or song. Some students at first cannot speak or sing while moving. At least they can join the movement and listen.

10. **Finally, as you use the activities in this book, keep in mind that you should also be participating in the activity and deriving increased understanding about students' abilities.** If we wish to be partners with students in their learning, we must first understand their *existing capabilities*. Then we can create opportunities for them to work with content, to use purposeful movement to develop an active learning base, to experience concepts in various ways, and to make connections to prior knowledge. We can help students take responsibility for their learning by asking them to work cooperatively with others, by encouraging them to make choices, by facilitating their thinking, by giving them the language to talk about movement and concepts, and by reflecting on experiences with them.

When active learning experiences are naturally undertaken and accompanied by teacher-facilitation, students are able to both understand and apply the concepts involved. **Active learning experiences + facilitation = ownership.**

Kindergarten and Above

Creativity

Awareness of personal space

Awareness of general space

Decision making

Expressing creativity in movement

Moving with objects

Moving in nonlocomotor ways

Moving in locomotor ways

Moving to music

Kindergarten and above

1 Creativity With Scarves

Each student has a scarf to use for nonlocomotor or locomotor movement. Students explore movement with their scarves. They move their scarves in personal space and then in general space, with or without music playing.

Materials

A scarf for each student

Optional: Recording of a slow selection from the *Rhythmically Moving* (RM) or *Changing Directions* (CD) series, such as *Gaelic Waltz* (RM1), *Hole in the Wall* (RM4), *At Va'ani* (CD1), or *Mîndrele* (CD6).

Activity to Experience

Each student selects a scarf and explores nonlocomotor (anchored) movement in personal space. Music is added if desired.

While most of the students use the scarves in their personal space, others may choose to move in general space, traveling between and around those in personal space. Several of the students's ideas may be noted, and other students may wish to try out those ideas.

All the students move in general space when they are ready to do so, watching that they do not bump into others. Music is added as desired. *Note: See Glossary for definitions of personal and general space.*

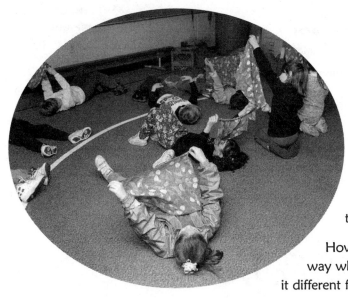

Facilitation and Reflection

When you were in your own personal space, what did you like to do with the scarf? (If students are unable to describe what they did, this provides an opportunity for the teacher to comment on what they were doing.)

How did you move your scarves in a different way when you moved about the room? How was it different from moving in personal space?

How might you move if you had paper plates or beanbags in your hands? How would your movements be different? (Ask second graders and above.)

What have you ever seen that moves like the scarves?

Extensions

Older students: Interact with partners while using the scarves. (They are not connected to their partners.)

Older students: Join together in a group, with each holding one end of a scarf while another person holds the other end. All move while connected in this way.

Older students: Small groups each create a movement score to one of the musical selections and then share their scores with the whole class. A class creative dance is choreographed using the input from the small groups of students.

The students may suggest other objects, such as paper plates, which can be used for creative movement. (See Activity 41.)

Key Experiences
in Movement
and Music

Moving with objects

Expressing creativity in movement

Describing movement

Exploring and identifying sounds

Kindergarten and above

2 Explore That Sound

Students explore ways to make sounds with bobbins, sticks, and other objects found in the classroom. They discuss the ways they moved and the sounds produced.

Materials

Bobbins (sometimes called quills), rhythm sticks, beanbags, and paper plates (or other sound-producing objects)

Activity to Experience

Students are given a pair of bobbins, sticks, or other objects; they then explore the sounds made by hitting or rubbing the objects together or by tapping their body or the floor with the objects.

Students share different sounds they discovered. Class members copy the way the student leader makes the sound.

Students talk about the sounds and make comparisons with sounds they have heard before.

Facilitation and Reflection

How did you make your sounds? Describe the movement you used.

Was anyone's sound a soft sound? A loud sound? How did you make it loud or soft?

How was Sally's sound different from Megan's sound? Was there anything about Tony's sound that was the same as Nathan's sound?

Are there objects at home that can make sounds? What would you do to make the sound?

Extensions

Guide the students to create patterns with the sounds, such as two taps of the sticks followed by two rubbing motions.

Help the students choose nonlocomotor or locomotor movements to accompany the sound. They continue this movement for as long as the leader makes the sound.

Use other objects, such as paper plates or unpitched percussion instruments (drums, maracas, finger cymbals), for sound exploration.

Play a mystery sound game. The leader chooses the object and makes the sound out of sight of the others. They guess what object is making the sound.

Explore sounds the voice, hands, or feet can make.

See Activity 54 for additional ideas to use with sounds.

Key Experiences
in Movement
and Music

Moving in nonlocomotor ways

Acting upon movement directions

Exploring the singing voice

Kindergarten and above

3 Low or High

Students work with the concepts of low and high by moving their bodies or parts of their bodies to these levels. They add low and high vocal sounds. They respond to the song's directions.

Materials

Music (see next page)

Activity to Experience

Students are encouraged to move their bodies to low and high levels. In each case, they identify where their bodies are placed. They add low and high voice sounds to match the body levels.

Students make a statue shape at a low level and at a high level.

As the song is sung, students respond to the song's directions.

Students are encouraged to think of body parts that can be placed low or high. For example, they may choose to solve the problem of how to place their feet at a high level.

Facilitation and Reflection

What can you say about movement and voice at a low level? A high level?

Describe your low-level statue shape. Your high-level statue shape.

How can you move your feet to a high level?

In our classroom what do we see at a low level? At a high level?

Extensions

Use the concept of middle level for movement exploration.

Encourage students to move with objects held at low and high levels.

Have students travel about the space with various parts of the body at low or high levels.

Also see Activity 10.

Low or High

Phyllis S. Weikart

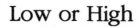

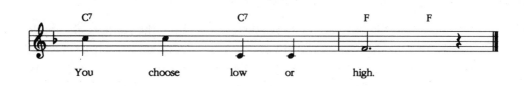

Voice and bo - dy way down low.

Voice and bo - dy way up high.

Make it low. Make it high.

You choose low or high.

Kindergarten and above

4 Musical Houses

Students use objects placed around the space as their "houses." They move in locomotor ways about the space when the music is playing and find a "house" when the music stops.

Materials

Objects for students to stand on or within, such as hoops, geometric shapes, carpet squares

Instrumental selection such as one of these from the *Rhythmically Moving* or *Changing Directions* series: *Hora Chadera* (CD1), *Hot Pretzels* (RM8), *Old Joe Clark* (RM1), *Sneaky Snake* (RM4)

Activity to Experience

Students explore ways to travel about the space without bumping into others or stepping on a "house." When the leader says "stop sign," all find a "house." To simplify the space-awareness task, begin with a few students moving at once.

Students step in place to the beat of the music, then travel about the space to the music. *(Note:* The younger students may not feel the beat or be able to keep it while traveling about the space. By second and third grade, you should see far more accuracy.) When the music stops, all stop. Students are encouraged to make a plan for traveling to a "house." All are encouraged to help others find the unoccupied "houses."

When the activity is repeated another day or continued the same day, a few "houses" are removed. Any student without a "house" is invited into another student's "house." No student should sit out, as in the traditional game of "Musical Chairs." Those pairs of students occupying particular "houses" together now travel as pairs, perhaps elbows touching.

Facilitation and Reflection

How did you keep yourself from bumping into others or stepping in other houses as you traveled without the music?

What locomotor movements did you use to travel to the music? Were some movements easier to use to stay in the beat?

What ways did you and your partner find to travel together after you ended up sharing a house?

Extensions

A student leader suggests a locomotor movement for all to use.

A student leader may also suggest an extension for the locomotor movement, such as marching with heavy feet.

Chairs may be used instead of the hoops or shapes or squares. Chairs are placed randomly about the space rather than in a row. Each person finds a chair or joins a partner on a chair.

Curriculum
Concepts

Steady beat

Accented syllables of names

Key Experiences
in Movement
and Music

Moving in nonlocomotor ways

Feeling and expressing steady beat

Kindergarten and above

5 Names in Beat

Students rock or pat the steady beat while seated in a circle, as they speak the first names of students in the class. Each rocking motion occurs on the accented syllable of a name.

Materials

None

Activity to Experience

Students are seated in a circle. They begin a rocking or patting motion, and match the word "ROCK" or "PAT" with their motion.

Several students volunteer to speak their names as they are naturally spoken. They start the rocking or patting, the teacher says "BEAT" at least four times to synchronize the movement, and each student leader in turn adds his or her name. All speak the names four to eight times. The endpoint of each rocking movement matches the accented syllable if a name has more than one syllable. In each of the following names, the normally accented syllable is in bold:

Er-ic	Ni-**cole**
Tim-othy	Cas-**san**-dra
E-**liz**-abeth	Alex-**an**-der

After several names are tried, the class may wish to recite two (or more) names four times each, without stopping between the different names.

Students may suggest saying the various names two times each or one time each.

Facilitation and Reflection

What does it mean to move in steady beat?

As we said Eric's name, when did the rock (pat) occur? (Ask the same about each of the other names used.)

Where would the rock occur on other words we know?

Extensions

Sing the name on one pitch. Change the pitch with each additional name.

Rock or pat and say each student's name one time. At first, say a name every other time you rock or pat. Then try to change the name on each rock or pat.

Make a chart of all the names with one syllable, two syllables, etc.

Sequence the names that students say by the number of syllables in each: Begin with a one-syllable name, then a two-syllable name, and so on.

Sequence the names by the placement of the accented syllable: Begin with names that have the accent on the first syllable, then those with the accent on the second syllable, and so on.

Also see Activity 23.

Curriculum
Concepts

Space awareness

Time awareness—start and stop

Key Experiences
in Movement
and Music

Moving in locomotor ways

Acting upon movement directions

Describing movement

Kindergarten and above

6 Stop Sign

Students explore locomotor movement as they travel about the space. They stop, without falling down, when the leader says the words "stop sign."

Materials

Locomotor movement menu written on a large sheet of cardboard (see right)

Optional: A cutout circle that is red on one side, green on the other side

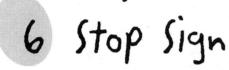

Locomotor Movement Menu

walk run

march tiptoe

jump hop

gallop slide

skip

Activity to Experience

Students are encouraged to find different ways to travel about the space by each selecting a locomotor movement from the menu. Several students volunteer to show how they are moving, and the others copy.

Students are encouraged to plan the way they are going to travel, to recall it afterward, and to describe different ways they were moving.

One student is the leader. That student says the word "go" (or shows the green side of the circle), and all travel about the space. When the student says "stop sign," or shows the red side of the circle, all stop and freeze without falling down.

The activity is continued with a new leader. The new leader may be encouraged to demonstrate a locomotor way to travel that all copy.

Facilitation and Reflection

What are some of the locomotor movements you used to travel about the space?

Who would like to show or tell us how you were moving? *Note:* If a student cannot use words to describe a movement, the teacher can ask others to describe the movement, or the teacher can comment on the movement.

What did you do to keep yourself from falling down when you heard the words "stop sign"?

What did you do to keep yourself from bumping into other students?

What are some other times when we might have to stop to keep from bumping others?

Extensions

The leader demonstrates or tells the group how to move.

The leader suggests not only the movement (march) but also the extension (with small steps).

The leader chooses a position for each person to balance in when they stop. (See Activity 33.)

Key Experiences
in Movement
and Music

Moving in locomotor ways

Acting upon movement directions

Describing movement

Kindergarten and above

7 Traveling Pathways Between Objects

Pairs of objects are placed in a pathway about the space. Students follow the pathway, traveling between each pair of objects.

Materials

Pairs of bobbins (8-inch quills) or other objects that can be set up in pairs, such as cones, paper cups, etc.

Activity to Experience

The pairs of bobbins (or other objects) to be used are set up about the space to create a pathway for traveling. The space between each pair of cones should be wide enough for the student to travel through easily. Different pathways are explored.

Students explore different ways to travel between the objects without knocking them down.

A student volunteers to be the leader. The followers travel in the same way the leader is traveling.

The pairs of bobbins may be placed closer together, creating a narrower pathway for more challenge.

Facilitation and Reflection

Describe how you traveled between the cones.

What did you have to think about so your feet didn't hit the cones?

What ways were easiest to travel when the cones were close together?

What other things do we travel between? (doorway, slats in a fence, tables in the classroom)

Extensions

Objects are set up by learners in three pathways (straight, curved, and zigzag). Three sections of the room are used for three groups of students. Each group takes one of the pathways and explores ways to travel. Groups change stations, so all explore the three pathways. The three groups talk about the different ways they liked to travel in the three pathways.

Other concepts, such as *around* and *over* or *outside* and *inside*, may be substituted for the concept of *between*. Students demonstrate the concept with the object. For additional experience with spatial concepts, see Activity 14.

Bobbins or other single objects may be placed in a pathway. The students travel so one leg steps on each side of the object and the object is between the legs.

Curriculum
Concepts
Attributes of shapes
Same and different

Key Experiences
in Movement
and Music
Moving with objects
Moving in locomotor ways
Acting upon movement directions
Exploring the singing voice

Kindergarten and above

8 Attributes of Shapes

Students travel to the shape that has the attribute given. They place a designated part of their body on that shape.

Materials

For each student, one geometric-shape cutout (with a nonskid surface) that is large enough to stand on

Optional: Recording of an instrumental selection, such as *Peat Fire Flame* (RM2) or *La Raspa* (RM3)

Activity to Experience

Shapes are placed about the space, and each student chooses a shape and stands on it. *Note:* They have had a prior discussion about the shapes and their attributes.

Students move about the space in the way selected by the student leader. When the leader says "stop sign," all return to a shape like the one they were on originally. Various students volunteer to each say one thing about their shape.

Students now go to a different shape, and each volunteers to say one thing about this new shape.

The activity continues with the leader saying or singing "stop sign" and then describing one attribute of a shape (e.g., "It has four corners"). This also could be sung. The leader also selects a body part to put on that shape (e.g., an elbow). Students travel to a shape that has the described attribute (four corners) and place the selected body part (their elbow) on it. (Several students may be on one shape.)

Facilitation and Reflection

What do you notice about the square? (four sides of equal length, four corners) About the rectangle? About the triangle?

How did you know you returned to a shape that was the same as the one you started on? How did you know you returned to a different shape?

What helped you find the shape the leader described?

What are some other shapes in this room that are the same as those we had on the floor? (chalkboard, doorway, window panes)

Extensions

The recording of *Peat Fire Flame* or *La Raspa* may be played. The students move about the space to the beat of the music. When the music stops, they freeze, then respond to the leader's directions for shape attribute and body part.

If the shapes have different colors, the group can respond to colors rather than to shape attributes.

Letters may be used instead of geometric shapes. For example, a student might look for a letter that has all curved lines (S), all straight lines (T), or a combination of curved and straight lines (D).

Kindergarten and above

9 Listening and Identifying

Students engage in a game of pointing with specific body parts to locations selected and described verbally by the leader.

Materials

None

Activity to Experience

Students explore pointing to various areas of the room with different parts of the body—with their elbow, thumb, toes, knee, etc.

Students are asked to think about what body part they would choose and where that body part should point. Then they see if they can verbally describe (not demonstrate) what they want someone to do.

Volunteers give the class verbal or sung directions for pointing with designated body parts to various locations in the room.

Facilitation and Reflection

What parts of your body did you find you could use for pointing?

What do you have to think about when you only tell, and don't show, what you want someone to do?

What are some other times when we should tell rather than show someone what we want them to do?

Extensions

Travel with locomotor movement, leading and pointing with a body part.

Sing or speak the directions, and also have the class identify whether the directions were sung or spoken.

A student points, using visual demonstration. The class identifies what body part is pointing and tries to determine where the leader is pointing.

Give students other opportunities to plan and give their classmates verbal or sung directions for nonlocomotor or locomotor movement.

Students lead the stages of movement for response with verbal directions. (See *Teaching Movement & Dance: A Sequential Approach to Rhythmic Movement* by Phyllis S. Weikart, pp. 20–27.)

Curriculum
Concepts

Space awareness—levels

Kinesthetic awareness

Thinking and language

Key Experiences
in Movement
and Music

Moving in locomotor ways

Describing movement

Kindergarten and above

10 Lively levels

Students explore levels for locomotor movement. While they are moving about the space, they talk about the levels they are using and what their bodies are doing to achieve those levels.

Materials

None

Activities to Experience

Students are engaged in a discussion about space awareness, including how to move in *levels*. (They have been introduced to levels with nonlocomotor movement prior to this experience.)

Students explore traveling in high, middle, and low levels. They are encouraged to talk about the locomotor movement they are using and the level represented.

Students volunteer to share their movements. The class members try out each leader's idea and talk about it, comparing and contrasting the various ideas presented.

Facilitation and Reflection

What do you remember about using levels for nonlocomotor (anchored) movement?

What did you discover about the levels as you were exploring locomotor (nonanchored) movement? Some of you were marching and others were tiptoeing and galloping.

What are some other times when
you might move at different levels? (walking through a
low doorway, jumping on a trampoline, getting into a car, climbing over a fence)

Extensions

Use the levels with nonlocomotor movement in different positions. Also see Activity 3.

Identify the levels when catching a ball.

Have the students plan their movements and the levels they will use.

Make a list of nonlocomotor and locomotor movements that can be performed easily at
the three levels.

Curriculum
Concepts

Space awareness—size of
movements

Planning

Kinesthetic awareness

Kindergarten and above

11 Planning to Step

Students explore locomotor movement with various-sized walking steps, jumps, and hops. They think about what they are going to do (make a plan) before they begin, and they verbalize their plan. They share their plan and action for others to copy.

Materials

None

Activity to Experience

Students explore locomotor movements using different sizes of those movements—big, medium, or little. Several volunteers share their ideas.

Students are encouraged to think about the movement and the size of the movement before they begin (to plan) and then to verbalize their plan. Practice time is given for students to try planning on their own.

Students in small groups each have a turn to tell the others in the group what they are going to do and to have the group members copy their idea. (The leader may tell his or her plan to the entire class.)

Facilitation and Reflection

What does it mean to move with movements of different sizes?

What locomotor movements did you like to use with big movements? With medium movements? With little movements?

How did you keep from bumping other students when you were using big movements?

When might you want to change the size of your movements?

Extensions

The planning process can be used for other extensions of locomotor and nonlocomotor movement as well as for combinations of extensions.

Kindergarten students can plan how they are going to travel to their area for work time.

Older students: Plan and tell the class what sequence of two locomotor movements they will use and what size each will be.

Curriculum
Concepts

Steady beat

Responding visually

Kinesthetic memory

Key Experiences
in Movement
and Music

Feeling and expressing steady beat

Moving in sequences to a common beat

Moving in locomotor ways

Acting upon movement directions

Moving to music

Kindergarten and above

12 Seven Jumps

Students jog in place to the recording and then follow the sequence of demonstrated movements to the longer and shorter held chords.

Materials

Recording of *Seven Jumps* (RM2)

Activity to Experience

Students listen to the music and jog in place to the steady beat. Older students or an adult leader may wish to lead 12 jogging steps plus one jump lasting four beats, for each of the melodies (16 beats each).

Longer and shorter chords follow the melody. One longer chord is added on each repeat of the music. Students are encouraged to volunteer a static (paused) movement for each prolonged chord that will be sequenced for the final performance. Eight static movements are needed for the entire selection. (Two static movements are used on the first playing of the music and then one is added on each repeat.)

Sample sequence of static movements:
1. Arms raised overhead
2. Hands to knees
3. Both arms out to the sides
4. One knee to the floor
5. Other knee to the floor
6. Both elbows to the floor

7. Lie face down in a push-up position

8. Roll to the back and kick legs in the air for final melody

(Source: Jennifer Weikart Danko)

Perform to the music as follows:

Melody: Run in place 12 steps; then do one jump held for four beats. Repeat.

Chords: On each of the two held chords, do the first two static movements (arms overhead, hands to knees). Return to the melody.

After the repeat of the jogging and jumping, add the third static movement (arms out to the sides) on the third chord.

Note: Add one more static movement from the list after the melody plays again.

Final melody: Lie on back, "bicycle" with arms and legs.

Facilitation and Reflection

How did you decide what movements to do on the longer chords?

How did you remember the sequence of movements?

Are there other times when we need to remember a sequence?

Extensions

Encourage the students to use all movements that require balance.

Develop and perform the sequence in small groups.

Travel about the space on the first melody. Add a balance for the final four beats of that melody. Repeat to the new melody.

Curriculum Concepts

Steady beat

Low-to-high and high-to-low vocal sounds

Key Experiences in Movement and Music

Moving in locomotor ways

Feeling and expressing steady beat

Exploring the singing voice

Kindergarten and above

13 People in Our Town

Students walk to a common beat and respond to the poem's directions. At the end of the poem, a low-high-low vocal sound is added.

Materials

There are <u>people</u> in **our** <u>town</u>
Going for a <u>walk</u> to**day.** _____
The **wind** is <u>blow</u>ing so **very** <u>hard,</u>
It **turns** us the <u>other</u> **way.** _____ Ooooh!

Activity to Experience

Students walk to the steady beat set by one of them. The student leader uses his or her internal tempo, and the class matches that beat. All use learner SAY & DO (WALK, WALK, WALK, WALK).

Students talk about the wind and what might happen if the wind blows very hard. The teacher shares the poem, after which students talk about what happens in the poem.

Students make siren-like vocal sounds, going from low to high to low while saying "Ooooh." They move their body in a direction that matches the sound.

One student is the leader. The teacher uses the **anchor word** "WALK" to bring all to group synchronization in the walking beat set by the student. The poem is added, with all walking to the steady beat. At the end, they turn around as they make the low-high-low vocal sound.

Categories of people or animals can be substituted for the word "people" in the poem. Students represent how those people or animals would walk.

Facilitation and Reflection

What happens when the wind blows gently or hard? How can we show it in our bodies?

How do we make our voices go low and high?

Extensions

Change the locomotor movement from walking to marching, galloping, or skipping.

Second-grade and older students can also walk a slower beat (microbeat).

Third-grade students can perform combinations of walking and patting (rocking), such as walking in the feet (microbeat) and patting in the hands (macrobeat).

Students perform sequences of movement to the poem.

Make up other poems that can accompany locomotor movement.

Curriculum
Concepts
Spatial concepts ("where" words)

Key Experiences
in Movement
and Music
Moving in nonlocomotor ways
Moving in locomotor ways
Expressing creativity in movement

Kindergarten and above

14 Understanding Spatial Concepts

Students explore nonlocomotor (anchored) and locomotor (nonanchored) movement using the list of spatial concepts developed by the students and teacher. They volunteer to share their ideas with the class.

Materials

Cards with words for spatial concepts (*over, under, through, between, around, up, behind*)

Optional, suggestion for extension: *Hole in the Wall* (RM4)

Activity to Experience

Students are assisted to develop a list of "where" words that can be expressed with movement. The final list is put on cards and placed so all can see it. (If you are working with kindergarten or first-grade students, you may wish to use "where" words and begin a list of them as you or the students introduce them.)

K–1 students: Cards are placed upside down.
One student draws a card, and all the students explore a way to express that word in movement. Volunteers share their movement ideas with the class, and the class copies.

Older students: Working with partners, students explore with nonlocomotor or locomotor movement any of the concepts they choose or the ones they draw at random from the cards. Partners talk about the spatial concept and choose a way to express it with either nonlocomotor or locomotor movement. Volunteers share their movement ideas, and the class copies and guesses what word they are representing.

Facilitation and Reflection

Describe the movement you used or others used.

What does the word "under" mean?

When is the concept *under* used in our class? (feet are under the tables, blocks are under the shelf)

Extensions

You may wish to have students draw and explore other awareness words such as "swing" and "push."

You may wish to create larger groups, so each group can design a choreography using a spatial concept.

Make a drawing of the way the concept was interpreted.

Students write sentences using the concepts as they were expressed in movement.

Put on a musical selection, such as *Hole in the Wall* (RM4), and have students move with a particular concept or a sequence of concepts.

Also see Activity 7.

Curriculum
Concepts

Space awareness

Steady beat

 Key Experiences
in Movement
and Music

Moving in locomotor ways

Feeling and expressing steady beat

Moving to music

Kindergarten and above

15 Who's Driving?

Paired students stand one behind the other. The student in front holds the steering wheel, and the student behind steers the car. Partners travel about the space; then music is added.

Materials

Recording of a selection with a good walking beat, such as those from the *Rhythmically Moving* or *Changing Directions* series, examples: *Korobushka* (RM8), *Santa Rita* (CD5), or *Sellinger's Round* (RM7)

Small hoops, paper plates, or Frisbees to simulate steering wheels (optional)

Activity to Experience

One half of the group holds both arms out in front, with or without a hoop, paper plate, or Frisbee, and walks about the space. The other half of the group then tries walking about the space with or without the hoop.

"Steering wheels" are passed out to half the group. Students with the steering wheels take partners who don't have them. Each student with a steering wheel stands in front of his or her partner. The partner behind holds the shoulders of the partner with the hoop and steers the partner about the space, avoiding contact with the others. Partners switch places and move again. *Note:* If "cars" collide, this is an "accident," and the two pairs of students involved sit down to wait for repair by the person designated to repair the cars.

Students all walk to the steady beat of the music. They exchange roles, form their "cars" again, and synchronize their steps to the music.

Facilitation and Reflection

What did you do to avoid bumping into the others?

What plan did you use if the partner in front was taller than the one behind?

When people drive cars, what safety rules do they have to follow?

Extensions

Each preschool or kindergarten student holds a small hoop, paper plate, or Frisbee and moves about the space.

Second-grade and older students may wish to try doing the same activity with the partners in front closing their eyes.

The partner behind responds to the way the partner in front is holding and turning the steering wheel or pretending to travel up and down hills (using the concepts of *pathway* and *level*).

Curriculum
Concepts
Visual responding
Same and *different*

Key Experiences
in Movement
and Music
Acting upon movement directions
Describing movement
Feeling and expressing steady beat

Kindergarten and above

16 Simon Says Variation

Students, in pairs, use both arms to explore static movements that are the "same" (symmetrical) or "different" (asymmetrical). Following a teacher's demonstration, a volunteer leader pats the knees three times with both hands simultaneously and follows this with a static "same" or "different" movement that the others copy and label.

Materials

None

Activity to Experience

Students take a partner and explore *same* and *different* arm movements that are static (paused). One partner is the leader, producing a movement that is either "the same" (symmetrical) or "different" (asymmetrical). The other partner follows and labels the movement "same" or "different."

The teacher leads the class by patting the knees three times and following this with a static, symmetrical movement (e.g., both hands on the shoulders). The class copies the pat and the paused movement after it, and labels the movement "same" or "different." The teacher leads again, this time doing an asymmetrical movement after the pats (one hand on the shoulder, the other on the knee). The classes copies and identifies the movement as "same" or "different."

Partners now take turns as leader and follower. The follower labels the movement as "same" or "different" after each person leads.

Several children volunteer to lead the entire class.

Facilitation and Reflection

What do we know about a movement that looks the same and a movement that looks different?

When do we see people using arm movements that are the same? Different? (different—reaching to turn off a light; same—reaching with both hands to remove an object from the top of a bookshelf)

Ask students to think of pairs of objects or two-sided objects (car headlights, statues, branches of a tree) and to consider whether they are the same or different.

Extensions

Use statue shapes instead of just arms.

Older students: See Activity 53.

Have the leader choose other places to pat symmetrically or asymmetrically.

Instead of *same* and *different*, use the words *symmetrical* and *asymmetrical*.

Instead of a static movement after the pats, use dynamic movements that keep going.

Kindergarten and above

17 We Keep the Beat Together

Students keep the steady beat to a song and then follow the visual demonstration performed by the leader.

Materials

We Keep the Beat Together on next page

Activity to Experience

One student leads the class with a walking tempo. All copy the leader. The teacher speaks the **anchor word** "WALK" eight times in the tempo the student has chosen. The song is sung with all keeping the beat. (See Activity 13 for an example of an anchor word.)

At the end of the song, all copy two single static movements selected by the leader.

Another student is the leader for the beat of the song. The new leader adds one movement to the two movements set by the first leader. The action song continues with new leaders and one new movement added each time. Here is a sequence of movements that might be used:

arms out in front of the body

thumbs up

knees bent

toes in

bottom out

head down

We Keep the Beat Together
(Go In and Out the Windows)

Adapted by Phyllis S. Weikart

Demonstrate "arms out," they copy.
Demonstrate "thumbs up," they copy.
With each repetition, add one more movement after
"arms out, thumbs up."

Facilitation and Reflection

How did you decide what movement to add when it was your turn to be the leader?

How did you remember the movements that were used before you were the leader?

Can you recall the order of all the movements?

Extensions

Have students work in small groups. Each group decides on a sequence of four to eight movements, which they do in their respective groups after the song.

Begin with fewer movements in the total sequence.

Substitute a learner SAY & DO echo for the watch and copy.

Also see Activities 12 and 13 for additional beat-keeping with locomotor movement.

Grade 1 and Above

Curriculum
Concepts

Even and *uneven*

Same and *different*

Key Experiences
in Movement
and Music

Describing movement

Expressing creativity in movement

Grade 1 and above

18 Is the Pattern Even or Uneven?

Groups of four explore locomotor movements that usually are done evenly and those usually done unevenly. The groups choose one of their even or uneven movements and add extensions of "where" and "how" to it.

Materials

None

Optional, suggestions for extension: *Jessie Polka* (RM8), *Yankee Doodle* (RM2), *Blackberry Quadrille* (RM2), or *Ersko Kolo* (RM4).

Activity to Experience

Students are asked to explore locomotor movements and to decide which ones could be called "even" and "uneven." They label locomotor movements on the chart as "even" or "uneven." *Note:* For grade 1, the curriculum concept of *uneven* refers to galloping, sliding, and skipping. For older children, an even movement might be running from one base to another; an uneven movement might be dodging people or objects while moving about the space.

Students form groups of four and share one of the ways they have chosen to move. Others in the group copy the leader and describe to the leader what they noticed as well as what the labels "even" and "uneven" mean to them.

> Locomotor
> Movement Menu
>
> walk run
> march tiptoe
> jump hop
> gallop slide
> skip

The groups choose a way to perform one of their movements with a "where" or "how" added, and some groups volunteer to present this to the class. Class members copy and describe these movements.

Groups of students create patterns of even and uneven movements and share them with the class.

Facilitation and Reflection

What makes a locomotor movement even or uneven?

How are these movements the same, and how are they different?

When you changed the "where" or "how," what did you do?

What types of patterns did you create?

Extensions

Move evenly and unevenly in nonlocomotor ways.

Move to music in the ways chosen. A suggestion for even patterns, such as marching or jumping, might be *Yankee Doodle* (RM2) or *Ersko Kolo* (RM4). Uneven patterns, such as galloping or skipping, might be performed to *Jessie Polka* (RM8) or *Blackberry Quadrille* (RM2).

Older students: Every 16 beats, change back and forth between even and uneven movements.

Curriculum
Concepts

Copying

Space awareness

Steady beat

Key Experiences
in Movement
and Music

Moving in nonlocomotor ways

Moving in locomotor ways

Acting upon movement directions

Feeling and expressing steady beat

Grade 1 and above

19 Statue Clones

Students work as partners. One student makes a statue shape while the music is playing. The other student travels about the space to the beat of the music. When the music stops, the student traveling returns to copy his or her partner's statue.

Materials

Recording of *Cherkessiya* (RM2), *Machar* (RM6), or other selection with a good walking beat.

Activity to Experience

Students explore different statue shapes, and all copy several students who volunteer to demonstrate their statues.

Working as partners, students copy each other's statue.

All listen to the recording and step in place to the steady beat. Then they travel about the space to the music.

When working in partners, one student is the statue and the other is the traveler. When the music is on, the statue partner freezes into a statue shape while the other travels about the space. When the music stops, all return to their partners and copy the partner's statue. The activity continues, with the partners changing their roles.

Facilitation and Reflection

What made a statue easy to copy? Hard to copy?

How did you keep from bumping into the statues or the other students who were traveling?

When might we see statue shapes?

Extensions

Younger students can move in a circle while the music is playing. The statue person, who is in the center, makes a statue when the music stops, and all copy.

Return to a different rather than the original partner.

This variation is for older students. When the statue is copied, the student who is copying makes the statue with one move at a time while talking about each movement.

Older students can keep one part of the statue moving to the steady beat of the music after the music stops.

Older students may decide to make a statue that mirrors their partner's statue or a statue that uses the same right and left body parts that their partner used.

Draw the statues, or title them and write a story about them.

Also see Activity 24.

Curriculum
Concepts

Representation

Visual discrimination

Key Experiences
in Movement
and Music

Moving in nonlocomotor ways

Moving in locomotor ways

Acting upon movement directions

Expressing creativity in movement

Grade 1 and above

20 Matching Stick-Figure Poses

Students create stick-figure poses on cards. A student leader selects one of the cards to show the class. The students try to strike the same pose with their bodies.

Materials

Cards with stick figures drawn on them, as shown here

    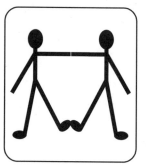

Activity to Experience

Students create stick-figure poses on cards. If the students cannot do this step, the stick figures might be made by a teacher or commercially made.

The student leader selects a card and shows it to the class. The class members construct with their bodies the pose shown on the card. They can be standing or lying down.

Students may wish to work in small groups, so more individuals have an opportunity to be the leader.

Facilitation and Reflection

What poses (shapes) were the easiest to copy? Why?

What poses (shapes) were the hardest to copy? Why?

Where might we see people in poses that we could copy? (statues and paintings in art museums, store mannequins, statues in the park, pictures in books)

Extensions

All might move around to the beat of the music. When the music stops, a card with a pose (shape) is shown and all copy.

Older students might draw stick figures that are joined in twos, threes, or fours.

The leader draws from among cards placed face down. After looking at the card, he or she gives the class only a verbal description of the pose (shape) on the card, and the class tries to figure out the pose. After the verbal description is given, the class looks at the card. This example also uses the key experience *describing movement*.

Curriculum
Concepts

Meaning of action words

Key Experiences
in Movement
and Music

Moving in nonlocomotor ways

Expressing creativity in movement

Describing movement

Grade 1 and above

21 Action Words

Ahead of time, students develop a list of action words, such as "shake," "punch," "dab," "flick," "float," and "touch." In this activity, they explore creative ways to express their words with movement.

Materials

None, or cards with action words written on them

Activity to Experience

Ahead of time, the teacher has students start a list of words that might be expressed in movement. Then, during the time stories are read to the students, the teacher can engage them in trying out movements reflecting the action words in the story.

After each student has explored his way to show "shake" (or other action word) several students volunteer to show their ways to the class, and the class copies these ideas.

Students talk about the different ways the action words were represented.

Facilitation and Reflection

What do we mean by the term "action words"?

What different body parts did you use to show the word "shake"?

What *different* ways did Suzie, Patrick, and Calista show the movement for "shake"?

When might you see people using a shaking motion?

Extensions

Place the action-word cards upside down in the middle of the space. Students draw a card and demonstrate their action word through movement. Volunteers share their words, and the class guesses what the word is.

Use the words in sentences, and act out the sentence.

Curriculum
Concepts

Representation

Locomotor and nonlocomotor
movement labels

Planning and recalling

Same and different

Key Experiences
in Movement
and Music

Moving in nonlocomotor ways

Moving in locomotor ways

Describing movement

Expressing creativity in movement

Grade 1 and above

22 Different Shape— Different Movement

Students in the gym choose and remember nonlocomotor movements they will perform on each of the geometric shapes. They plan which locomotor movement to use to travel from one shape to another.

Materials

Geometric-shape cutouts with nonskid backing (circle, square, rectangle, triangle)

Nonlocomotor movement menu written on a large sheet of cardboard (see below).

Optional, suggestion for extension: musical selection such as *Sauerländer Quadrille* (CD3) or *Pata Pata* (RM6)

Activity to Experience

Geometric shapes are placed about the space with equal numbers of each of the four shapes. Each student stands on or next to one of the geometric shapes.

Students agree on four nonlocomotor movements they will use with each of the geometric shapes, such as twist for the square and swing for the triangle. They use the menu of nonlocomotor movement.

Students perform the nonlocomotor movements for the shapes they are standing on or next to. They are encouraged to talk about how they are doing the movement agreed upon for each shape (e.g., twisting arms overhead or to the side).

Nonlocomotor Movement Menu	
bend	straighten
twist	turn
swing	rock
curl	stretch
push	pull
rise	fall

Students plan how they are going to travel to another shape (same or different) that they have selected. They travel to that shape and recall the movement that accompanies that shape.

Facilitation and Reflection

Describe how you are doing your twisting (swinging) movement. Where are you doing it?

What helped you remember the movement to do on the shape you selected?

Where in the room do you see those shapes?

Extensions

Older students: Put the shapes in a row on the floor, and decide on a sequence of movements to do with the shapes. See Activity 77.

Older students: Decide on locomotor or integrated movements for each of the shapes.

Move to the beat of a recorded musical selection, such as *Sauerländer Quadrille* (CD3) or *Pata Pata* (RM6).

Curriculum
Concepts

Steady beat

Companion words

Key Experiences
in Movement
and Music

Moving in nonlocomotor ways

Feeling and expressing steady beat

Grade 1 and above

23 Combining Words

Students generate a list of two-word combinations. They speak the two words separately with each rocking motion.

Materials

None

Activity to Experience

Students practice rocking together on a common beat. They might form a circle made up of the entire class, smaller circles, lines, or partners. They use learner SAY & DO with the word "ROCK."

Students work with a list of two-word combinations they have generated. Each endpoint of the rocking movement is united with the combination of the two words, such as "teddy bear," "falling snow," or "soccer game." The "X" and the bold syllable indicate the endpoint of the rock. *Words flow together and are spoken naturally.* One student sets the rocking beat for all to follow. The rocking movement can be side-to-side or front-to-back. See figure below.

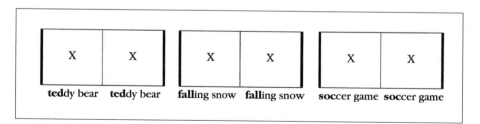

For rocking and saying the word combinations, students may suggest using a standing position alone, or having several students stand joined together with an object, such as a pole.

Facilitation and Reflection

How do you get the words to flow together?

What are other examples of combining words?

Extensions

Extend word combinations into word phrases, such as "cuddly teddy bears." This phrase would have one rock for "cuddly teddy" and another rock for "bears," as shown at right.

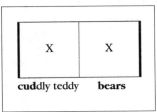

Sing two pitches with the two words (music key experience: *developing melody*).

Also see Activity 5.

Curriculum
Concepts

Kinesthetic memory

Steady beat

Same and different

Planning and recalling

Key Experiences
in Movement
and Music

Moving in nonlocomotor ways

Moving in locomotor ways

Acting upon movement directions

Describing movement

Feeling and expressing steady beat

Moving to music

Grade 1 and above

24 Statues That Change

One student makes a statue shape, which is copied by a partner. The copier travels around the space to the music, and the statue-maker alters the statue with one change. The copier returns and copies the statue again, identifying the one change that has been made.

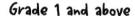

Materials

Recording of an instrumental selection, such as *Peat Fire Flame* (RM2) or *Soldier's Joy* (RM2)

Activity to Experience

The class breaks into pairs. One person in each pair makes a statue shape, which the partner copies. Copiers are encouraged to talk about the statue shapes.

Copiers tell their partners how they are going to travel about the space to the beat of the music, and then they begin. While the partners are traveling, each statue-maker creates one change in his or her statue. When the music stops, the travelers return to their partner and copy the partner's new statue, identifying the one change that was made in it.

Partners reverse roles.

Note: This activity might also be carried out without music.

Facilitation and Reflection

What was special about your partner's statue?

As the statue-maker, how did you decide on the change you would make in your statue?

If you were the copier, how could you tell what change your partner made in the statue? How did you remember the way the statue was made?

Was there anything about the music that helped you choose the way you would travel?

Extensions

Kindergarten: Partners are selected. One student makes a statue. Partner copies. The copier, using hands-on guidance, makes one change in the student's statue. The statue-maker identifies the change.

When working with kindergarten students, you may wish to first have one statue-maker to whom all respond. See Activity 19.

Create more than one change in the statue.

The statue-maker tells the copier the one change to make when he or she returns, but the statue-maker does not demonstrate the change.

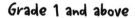

Key Experiences
in Movement
and Music

Acting upon movement directions

Feeling and expressing steady beat

Moving in nonlocomotor ways

Grade 1 and above

25 Beat Echo

Students respond in steady beat to the leader's movements. The response occurs after the leader performs the single movement two times. Music is added.

Materials

Recording of *Echo* (RM1)

Activity to Experience

Students try out single movements *in repetition* using steady beat, such as patting their knees or shoulders, pushing their arms away from their body, pounding with both fists, etc. Using learner SAY & DO helps children keep the beat steady.

Students try a series of movements, with each movement performed two times in a slow, steady beat (e.g., patting knees twice, patting shoulders twice, pushing twice, and pounding twice).

The class reviews the concept of *echo* movement (in which followers do the movement after the leader finishes, not while the leader is moving). The teacher leads several examples like the one shown to the right.

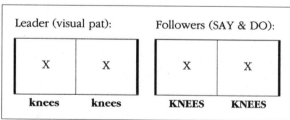

One student volunteers to lead the class or small group. The leader performs the first movement two times in steady beat, and the class copies (echoes). This sequence is repeated. Then the second movement is led two times, followed by the echo. This sequence is repeated. If the response is performed with learner SAY & DO, it will be more accurate.

Other students volunteer to be the leader.

Music is added, and the rocking beat tempo is used for each set of movements, as shown at right.

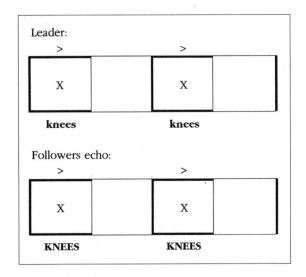

Facilitation and Reflection

What does it mean to move in steady rocking beat to the music?

What does the word "echo" mean?

When you were the one to echo the movement, how did you know when to begin?

When you were the leader, how did you know when to begin the second pair of movements?

Are there any other times you might hear an echo or use the idea of *echo*?

Extensions

Use single locomotor or integrated movements instead of nonlocomotor movements.

Older students: The leader performs two locomotor movements followed by two nonlocomotor movements before the class or group echoes, such as two jumps and two pats of the shoulders. For a challenge, try alternating the locomotor movement with the nonlocomotor movement (hop, snap, hop, snap). Marching beat tempo is used.

The leader speaks the labels for the movement, and the class echoes with SAY & DO.

The followers echo the movements of the *body scale,* with the corresponding pitches sung on a neutral syllable. (Please refer to *Foundations in Elementary Education: Music* by Elizabeth B. Carlton and Phyllis S. Weikart, p. 35, for an explanation of the *body scale.)*

See also Activities 26 amd 64.

Curriculum
Concepts

Sequence

Echo

Musical phrase

Key Experiences
in Movement
and Music

Moving in nonlocomotor ways

Moving in sequences to a common bea[

Feeling and expressing steady beat

Moving to music

Grade 1 and above

26 Echo Sequence

Students explore two-movement sequences. Volunteers lead a partner, and then the class, in echo movement. Music is added if desired.

Materials

Recording of an instrumental selection, such as *Echo* (RM1), *Road to the Isles* (RM5), or *Troika* (RM2)

Activity to Experience

Students explore two-movement sequences, such as *pat knees, pat shoulders* (KNEES, SHOULDERS); or *straighten both arms, then bend them* (STRAIGHT, BEND).

Students recall the concept of *echo movement*. The teacher leads several examples of two-movement sequences, like the one shown below, and the class copies after the teacher completes the second movement of each sequence. A strategy of using WHISPER & DO while the leader is moving and then SAY & DO when copying helps learners to experience success.

Each student works with a partner. One person is the leader and the other is the copier with echo movement. They change roles after several sequences are copied and repeated.

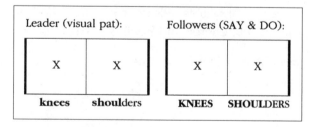

Leader (visual pat):		Followers (SAY & DO):	
X	X	X	X
knees	**shoulders**	**KNEES**	**SHOULDERS**

Partners volunteer to lead the class in these echo movement sequences. *(Note: If the leader* repeats the sequence a second time after it is echoed, rather than immediately using a new sequence, more students will be successful and the student does not have to plan new sequences with each lead.)

Music is added, and the macrobeat is used, as shown below. Students identify the beginning of the phrase for the start of each movement sequence. As movements are led, echoed, and then repeated, the form of the music also is experienced.

Facilitation and Reflection

What do we mean by a *movement sequence?* Describe one you used.

What does it mean to *echo?* What are some other occasions when the echo concept is used?

How do you know when to begin your turn when you echo the leader?

How did you remember the sequence performed by the leader?

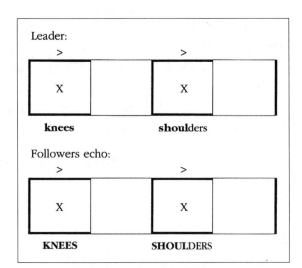

Extensions

Lead single movements instead of sequenced ones. See Activities 37 and 64.

Use locomotor movement or integrated movement for the echo sequence.

Combine one locomotor movement with one nonlocomotor movement in the sequence (JUMP, CLAP).

Note: Try this activity without music. Person echoing does so in the same timing as the leader.

Key Experiences
in Movement
and Music

Moving in nonlocomotor ways

Moving in locomotor ways

Expressing creativity in movement

Describing movement

Grade 1 and above

27 Extending Our Movements

Students review several basic nonlocomotor and locomotor movements. They talk about and explore ways to extend those movements using **direction, level, pathway, intensity, size,** *and* **flow.** *They share their extensions with the class.*

Materials

Menu of nonlocomotor movement extensions that students have recalled, written on a large sheet of cardboard (shown at right)

Activity to Experience

Students choose several basic nonlocomotor or locomotor move-
ments and recall the body-awareness concepts for those labels. The class reviews several of the movements chosen.

Students discuss ways to extend (vary) those movements. They try several extensions that they want to use with one of their movements. Students volunteer to share their ideas.

Students explore whether or not the extensions chosen can be used with other movements.

The class reflects on the extensions tried and their applicability to a variety of nonlocomotor and locomotor movements.

Nonlocomotor-
Locomotor
Movement
Extensions Menu
direction   level
pathway   size
intensity   flow
time

Facilitation and Reflection

What are some of the nonlocomotor movements we have explored in other class periods?

What are some of the locomotor movements?

What ways can we make those movements different?

How are *direction*, *level*, *pathway*, etc., different if we use them with nonlocomotor movement instead of locomotor movement?

When might we use *direction*, *level*, *pathway*, etc., other than in this class?

Extensions

Students can pick extensions from cards placed face down in the center of the floor and also pick the movement to use for that extension.

All students can work with one movement and one extension and then share the different ways they found to perform that movement with its extension.

A student may do a movement with one or more extensions. The class copies, then identifies the extension(s) used.

For further extensions of nonlocomotor and locomotor movement, see Activities 10, 11, 28, and 35.

Key Experiences
in Movement
and Music

Moving in nonlocomotor ways

Expressing creativity in movement

Acting upon movement directions

Grade 1 and above

28 Making Pathways in the Air

Students explore and identify nonlocomotor movement pathways. They discover what types of pathways are created by different nonlocomotor movements.

Materials

Large sheets of paper, yarn

Cards illustrating the three pathways (shown at left)

Activity to Experience

Students explore the pathways they make using nonlocomotor (anchored) movement and share their ideas with the class. They discuss various nonlocomotor movements and decide what pathways the movements usually follow.

Students, working in small groups, draw pathways on large sheets of paper and then also use yarn to represent pathways. *Note:* All three kinds of pathways (straight, curved, and zigzag) can be part of the drawings and the yarn representations. In moving body parts along the pathways they represented, students create a movement score. They are encouraged to share their ideas.

Facilitation and Reflection

What do you already know about pathways? What are the basic pathways?

Describe the pathway you drew and represented with the yarn.

What movement did you choose to represent your pathway and why?

What kinds of pathways are used in writing letters? In making drawings? In writing music?

What pathways do you see represented in our classroom?

Extensions

Students add vocal sounds to represent their movement score.

Different body parts may represent the nonlocomotor movement when each pathway changes.

Students construct pathways used to make capital letters. They move some body part along the pathway for each letter selected, choosing the type of movement they will use to represent each type of pathway.

Students may choose to draw pathways, including letters, on the backs of partners, using two pointer fingers joined. The partner identifies the pathway and replicates it in the air, in front of his or her body, the same way it was drawn on the back. Also refer to Activity 44.

Pathways may be extended to locomotor movement. See Activity 7.

Students can "sing" the pathway on random pitches (music key experience: *exploring the singing voice).*

Key Experiences
in Movement
and Music

Moving in nonlocomotor ways

Feeling and expressing steady beat

Singing alone and in groups

Grade 1 and above

29 Is It Macrobeat or Microbeat?

Students detect if the movement response to rhymes, songs, and recordings is on the macrobeat or the microbeat. They demonstrate the beat chosen in a different way and in the opposite way.

Materials

Rhymes and songs students know

Recordings of instrumental selections, such as *Hora Chadera* (CD1), *Yankee Doodle* (RM2), *Milanovo Kolo* (CD3), or *Sham Hareh Golan* (RM9)

Activity to Experience

Students recall the difference between *macrobeat* and *microbeat* as they listen to or say rhymes, sing songs, and listen to recorded selections. (See Glossary for definitions of *microbeat* and *macrobeat*.)

One student volunteers to leave the room to be the "beat detective." The class selects a rhyme or song they know and decides whether to keep the macrobeat or the microbeat. They say the rhyme or sing the song, keeping the beat they have chosen. The "beat detective" returns, copies and identifies the beat, then keeps that same beat with a different movement. The "beat detective" then demonstrates a movement in the beat not chosen by the class.

The game also is played with recorded selections identified.

Small groups can play the game, so more students have a turn as the beat detective.

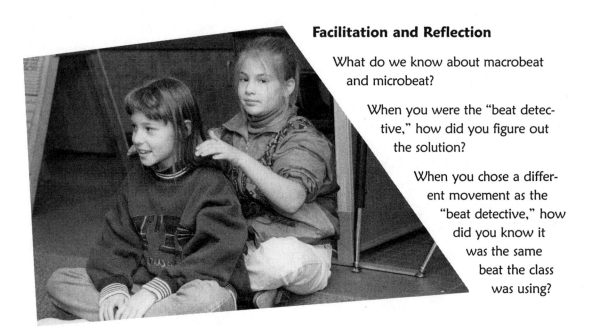

Facilitation and Reflection

What do we know about macrobeat and microbeat?

When you were the "beat detective," how did you figure out the solution?

When you chose a different movement as the "beat detective," how did you know it was the same beat the class was using?

Extensions

Second grade and above: Use locomotor movement for the "beat detective" game.

Third grade and above: Review folk dances and decide what parts of the dance use macrobeat and what parts use microbeat.

Choreograph movement sequences to rhymes, songs, or recorded selections using macrobeat and microbeat. Example: Walk four microbeats followed by two macrobeats, or walk six microbeats followed by one macrobeat, or jump three macrobeats and hop two microbeats.

For older students, try Activity 76 or 81.

Curriculum
Concepts
Responding to visual cues
Kinesthetic awareness

Key Experiences
in Movement
and Music
Moving in nonlocomotor ways
Acting upon movement directions
Describing movement

Grade 1 and above

30 Puppets

One student leads single static movement by moving a "puppet" who has eyes closed, using hands-on guidance to give movement directions.

Materials

None

Activity to Experience

Each student has a partner and one in each pair is the leader. Partner A closes his or her eyes so he or she is the "puppet" and partner B is the leader. Both are standing. Partner B moves partner A, one movement at a time, with the puppet identifying each move.

After all have explored the two roles, one pair volunteers to lead the class. Each move that the lead pair makes is copied by the class, also working in pairs. Puppets tell their partners about each move.

A different pair volunteers to lead the class, and partners A and B in each pair change roles.

Facilitation and Reflection

As the puppet, which movements were the most comfortable and the easiest to identify? Which were the hardest?

If you did this activity with the puppet seated, what different things did you have to think about?

What different ways can the arm move at the shoulder? At the elbow?

Extensions

Use verbal directions for the partner to respond to. *See Activity 47.*

Use two or more movements before the partner responds.

All move their partners to the phrases of a musical selection. The single movement occurs at the beginning of each phrase.

Note: This activity was initiated by students in a classroom where there was a visually impaired student. The student learned new movements by following a partner's hands-on guidance (no verbal directions were given) as the teacher or student leader demonstrated the movements.

Also see Activity 52 for more responding to visual cues.

Curriculum Concepts

The concepts *push* and *up*

AB form *(see Foundations in Elementary Education: Music,* by Elizabeth B. Carlton and Phyllis S. Weikart, p. 65

Key Experiences in Movement and Music

Moving in nonlocomotor ways

Expressing creativity in movement

Moving to music

Labeling form

Grade 1 and above

31 Pushing Up

*Students explore the concepts of **push** and **up**. They devise as many ways as possible to unite the two concepts into push-ups. Small groups have an opportunity to share their discoveries. A choreography to music results from the ideas presented.*

Materials

None

Recordings of selections with a moderate tempo, such as *Dŭcec* (RM8) or *Armenian Misirlou* (RM9)

Activity to Experience

Students work with the two concepts of *push* and *up*—the nonlocomotor movement plus directional extension. They explore these concepts in many different ways, sharing their ideas.

Small groups are formed, and students unite the words into *push-ups*. They create different ways to show the concept. They share their ideas with the class.

Students try their push-up ideas to music. Several ideas are decided on, and the class performs the push-up choreography using the two main sections of the music (AB form). The class changes their movement each time the music changes from A to B or B to A. (Each section has 16 microbeats.)

Facilitation and Reflection

What did you do to show the word "push"? The word "up"?

What different ways did you find to connect the idea of *push* and the idea of *up?*

How were the group's push-up movements different? The same?

When might we use the idea of push-up? (raising a window, doing exercises)

Extensions

Combine other directional concepts with *push* (such as *push down, push out, push away)* or with *up* (such as *swing up, jump up).*

Students think of other action words that can be combined with directional words (e.g., *punch away).*

Also see Activity 21.

Older students create sequences of action words combined with directional concepts (e.g., *push up, push down, shake in front, shake to the side).*

Key Experiences
in Movement
and Music

Moving in nonlocomotor ways

Describing movement

Acting upon movement directions

Grade 1 and above

32 Recalling the Past

Students discuss strategies they might use to recall movements that have occurred. They explore nonlocomotor movements in different directions. Selecting an order for the movement directions, they perform them and then recall the order of the directions.

Materials

None

Activity to Experience

Students are encouraged to try nonlocomotor (anchored) movements with their arms outstretched in different directions, such as twisting their arms forward, sideward, upward, or downward.

Students recall what arm directions they used for their nonlocomotor movements.

Students now work with one nonlocomotor movement and decide on an order of the directional variations for the movement. They are encouraged to think about how they are performing their movements, so they can recall the order they used.

Students volunteer to show the class how they performed their movements. (Class joins in with the demonstration.) The leader then recalls for the class how the movement was performed. The class determines if the recall has been accurate.

Facilitation and Reflection

What different arm directions did you use for the movement?

What helped you to recall how you performed your movements?

When might we be asked to recall the order of actions we have just completed?

Extensions

Have students recall sequences of movements, such as three hops, one jump, and five walks.

Have students recall a four-motion sequence of single actions that will be repeated several times, such as straightening arms in front, touching shoulders, touching knees, and bending arms.

Older students recall the sequence of movements in a dance.

Also see Activity 47.

Key Experiences
in Movement
and Music

Moving in locomotor ways

Feeling and expressing steady beat

Acting upon movement directions

Moving to music

Grade 1 and above

33 Stop and Balance

Students decide on locomotor movements to synchronize to the steady beat of the music. When the music stops, they copy the balanced position of the leader.

Materials

Locomotor movement "menu" (from Activity 6)

Recording of an instrumental selection, such as *La Raspa* (RM3) or *Les Saluts* (RM1)

Optional: Drum for extension

Activity to Experience

Students explore different ways to move about the space and to stop in different balanced positions.

Several students volunteer to be the leader. They share their ways of moving and balancing. When they want the class to stop and balance, they say the words "stop sign." The leader is responsible for starting and stopping the music.

Students listen to the recording, step to the beat in place, and then explore different locomotor movements the music suggests to them.

A new leader continues the activity.

Facilitation and Reflection

What type of stopping position made it easy to balance? Hard to balance?

When might you have to stop suddenly and not fall down?
(if a car was approaching, or if someone moved in front of you and you were not expecting it)

Extensions

Kindergarten students will enjoy Activity 6, which is a simplified version of this activity.

Grade 3 and above: Using a drum or other hand-held instrument, the leader keeps the same beat of the music after the music pauses. All find a way to move some part of their body to the leader's beat while keeping their balanced position.

Curriculum Concepts

Steady beat (*macrobeat* and *microbeat*—see Glossary)

Space awareness

Musical form

Key Experiences in Movement and Music

Moving in locomotor ways

Moving in nonlocomotor ways

Feeling and expressing steady beat

Moving to music

Labeling form

Grade 1 and above

34 Trains

Students march in trains to the music. During the A section (first melody), the leader faces the others in the train and uses both arms to lead macrobeat movements. During the B section (second melody) the leader travels about the space in microbeat, with the train joined behind.

Materials

Recording of an instrumental selection, such as *Korobushka* (RM8) or *Tzadik Katamar* (CD2)

Optional, suggestion for extension: *Gaelic Waltz* (RM1) or *Tipsy* (RM6)

Activity to Experience

Students listen to the music and march about the space. They also explore doing movements with their arms to the *macrobeat* while standing in personal space.

Trains of students join together. Each student places both hands on the shoulders of the student in front. They practice marching about the space, giving each student a chance to be the leader. They also practice leading arm movements in macrobeat. Two **simplify** strategies are (1) to begin alone or with shorter trains and (2) to have the students form parades without hands on the shoulders.

The first leader, with both arms, leads nonlocomotor movements to the *macrobeat* on the single A section of the music. On the B sections, the leader leads the train about the space, marching to the **microbeat** of the B sections. At the end of the two B sections, the leader goes to the end of the train, leaving the second person as the new leader. The form of the music is ABB.

Facilitation and Reflection

What arm movements did you use for the macrobeat of the music?

What did you do to avoid other trains in the space?

What helped you know when to change from the A section to the B section of the music and when to go to the end of the train?

Extensions

Grade 3 and above: Choose which beat to use and keep it with arms and legs while traveling in the trains. If one arm keeps the beat, the trains can be joined with the other hand. If both arms are used, the trains cannot be joined.

Experiences that precede this include moving alone; moving in pairs, one behind the other and not joined, and then joined; progressing to longer trains; and pausing the music for change of leaders.

Grade 2 and above: Put paper plates under both feet and "skate" to the macrobeat. The recordings *Gaelic Waltz* (RM1) or *Tipsy* (RM6) work well for this.

Key Experiences
in Movement
and Music

Moving in locomotor ways

Acting upon movement directions

Describing movement

Moving to music

Grade 1 and above

35 Traveling Pathways Without Objects

Students decide on three different locomotor movements to represent each of the three pathways—curved, straight, and zigzag (angle). They respond to a representation of the pathway drawn by one of the students.

Materials

Cards and a marker

Optional, suggestions for extensions: Recording of an instrumental selection, such as *Zigeunerpolka* (RM2) or *Sliding* (RM1); recording of a selection in AABB form, such as *Rakes of Mallow* (RM2) or *Irish Washerwoman* (RM3)

Activity to Experience

Students review the three kinds of pathways (straight, curved, zigzag, or angle), and explore movements for each kind. They share by describing their pathway and showing the movement they used. All copy the leader's movement and pathway.

A volunteer is given a card and a marker and asked to draw a pathway on the card and to show the movement for the pathway. The followers name the pathway and the movement and perform that movement.

A beginning strategy: Have the three kinds of pathways drawn on cards prior to the activity. The student leader chooses the card, names the pathway, and shows the movement for all to copy.

Facilitation and Reflection

How are the three pathways different?

What movements did you like to use to represent a straight pathway? A curved pathway? A zigzag pathway?

How could you use movement in other ways to show these three kinds of pathways?

How could the entire class move together to show these pathways?

Extensions

Older students may wish to make the movement more complex by adding an extension to the movement chosen, such as level, intensity, direction, size, or timing.

Objects may be used to construct pathways. See Activity 7.

The three kinds of pathways may be chosen to represent each section of the three-part musical selection *Zigeunerpolka* (RM2) or *Sliding* (RM1). Decide how many times each movement will be done to correspond to each section of the music. (There are 16 microbeats in each section.) This extension involves the music key experience *labeling form*.

The movement may change as sections of the music repeat or change. Example: Using music in AABB form, such as *Rakes of Mallow* (RM2) or *Irish Washerwoman* (RM3), students select locomotor movement and the pathway for the first A section; add an extension such as change of level, intensity, or size of step for the second A section; choose a different movement and pathway for the B section; and add an extension for the repeat of the B section. The same locomotor movements, with different extensions, may be chosen for later repetitions of the melody.

Curriculum
Concepts

Classification

Locomotor movement extensions

Steady beat

Key Experiences
in Movement
and Music

Moving in locomotor ways

Acting upon movement directions

Feeling and expressing steady beat

Moving to music

Grade 1 and above

36 Who Matches Me?

Students choose a locomotor movement and begin to move about the space. While moving, they find one student or several who are doing the same locomotor movement. They move together, matching one another's timing. They then decide on one extension of their locomotor movement and perform it for the class.

Materials

Optional, suggestion for extension: Recording of an instrumental selection, such as *Cherkessiya* (RM2), *Man in the Hay* (RM3), or *Milanovo Kolo* (CD3)

Activity to Experience

Students are encouraged to try out various locomotor (nonanchored) movements and to choose one they will use.

All students begin to move using their chosen locomotor movements. They look around as they are traveling and find one or more persons doing the same locomotor movement.

Students, grouped by locomotor movement, find a way to match one another's movement and timing. Each group demonstrates for the class.

Subgroups within each locomotor movement (two or three people) decide on one extension for their movement, such as direction, level, pathway, intensity, or size, and synchronize their locomotor movement using this extension.

Groups volunteer to demonstrate for the class. The class copies and identifies the extension.

Facilitation and Reflection

What are the locomotor (nonanchored) movements we could demonstrate?

When we are traveling using our own locomotor movement, what do we look for to make a match?

What strategies can we use to match one another's timing?

When could we use these extensions in other situations?

Extensions

Begin with the locomotor movement plus one extension, and have the students find someone using the same.

Travel to the beat of a recorded selection, such as *Cherkessiya* (RM2), *Man in the Hay* (RM3), or *Milanovo Kolo* (CD3).

Make a chart of all the combinations used.

Curriculum
Concepts

Number representation

Balance

Key Experiences
in Movement
and Music

Moving in nonlocomotor ways

Acting upon movement directions

Describing movement

Grade 1 and above

37 Numbers and Statue Shapes

Students draw a card with one to six dots on it. They make a balanced statue shape with the same number of body parts touching the floor as represented by the dots on the card. They describe their shapes.

Materials

A set of cards, each bearing 1 to 6 dots (one card for each student)

Activity to Experience

Cards with dots on them are randomly handed out to all the students in the class.

According to the number of dots on the card, each student forms a balanced statue shape with that number of body parts touching the floor.

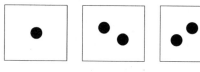

Volunteers are given an opportunity to describe their shapes.

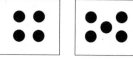

Students may wish to take a partner to make a combined shape that either represents the number of dots on one card or the total number of dots on their two cards.

Facilitation and Reflection

How did you decide which body parts to place on the floor so you would not lose your balance?

How did you decide on the order in which you placed the body parts on the floor to maintain balance?

In what other ways could you represent the numbers on your cards?

Extensions

Reverse the process. One student makes a statue shape. The partner then identifies the number and makes a different statue shape with that number of body parts touching the floor.

Grade 2 and older: Use nonlocomotor or locomotor movement to represent the number shown by the dots. Four dots on the card could be represented with four twists. The person doing the representing uses learner SAY & DO, "TWIST, TWIST, TWIST, TWIST," rather than counting to 4.

For other statue-shape activities, refer to Activities 19 and 24.

Key Experiences
in Movement
and Music

Moving in nonlocomotor ways

Acting upon movement directions

Describing movement

Grade 1 and above

38 How Many Points of Contact?

Working in pairs, students determine the total number of body parts that are in contact with the floor as the partners copy each other's statue shape.

Materials

None

Activity to Experience

Students work with partners and explore statue shapes having varying numbers of parts of the body in contact with the floor. *Note:* You may wish to limit the number of body parts any one statue has in contact with the floor to no more than 15. The foot counts as one body part, and the *full* hand counts as one body part, unless only some fingers touch the floor; then the fingers can be counted individually.

One student makes a statue shape. The partner copies the statue shape one section at a time, and adds together the number of body parts as they are put in contact with the floor. Example: "I began with 1 foot on the floor plus 1 knee, which equals 2 parts. Then 2 elbows make 4, and 1 hand makes 5. Adding the 3 fingers of the other hand gives me 8 body parts touching the floor."

The partner now is the leader in making a different statue.

Facilitation and Reflection

In making your statue, how did you decide which and how many body parts should touch the floor?

How did you decide the order in which to build your statue when you were copying your partner?

What are some other times when you add things up the way you added up the body parts touching the floor?

Extensions

The follower establishes the total number of body parts in contact with the floor, makes the statue, and then begins to remove body parts from the floor, thus subtracting and yet trying to maintain balance.

Three or four students are in a group. All but one student makes a statue shape. The student responding identifies the number of floor-contact body parts for the first statue and then adds to that the total for the next statue, etc. Now the responder makes a statue with that total number of body parts on the floor. *Note:* Each statue would need to be given a limit, so the total for the three or four successive statues would not exceed 15.

Students can respond to the *greater than* (>) and *less than* (<) symbols, with one student making the same statue shape as another student, but with a different number of body parts touching the floor. For example, if the first student makes a statue shape with 9 parts touching the floor, the second student might use the *less than* symbol to show that his or her statue shape has 7 parts touching the floor and that 7 < 9.

Curriculum
Concepts

Patterning

Striking

Musical phrase

Musical form

Key Experiences
in Movement
and Music

Moving with objects

Feeling and expressing steady beat

Moving in sequences to a common bea[t]

Moving to music

Grade 1 and above

39 Beat-Keeping With Mallets

Students work with the progression of basic mallet sequencing to establish easier to more difficult patterns.

Materials

One pair of mallets or rhythm sticks and four sturdy paper plates per student

Optional, suggestion for extension: Recording of an instrumental selection, such as *Popcorn* (RM7) or *Hadarim* (CD4)

Activity to Experience

Two of the paper plates are lined up side-by-side, upside down. Students explore hitting the two paper plates with the mallets in single symmetrical movements.

One student sets the beat, and all work with the single movement of hitting the two plates simultaneously. (For music educators, this is a lead-up to students playing a bordun on a barred instrument.)

Students alternate hitting one paper plate and then the other, following one student's lead (a lead-up to a broken bordun).

Students line up four plates side-by-side for sequenced mallet movements.

Different patterns are led by the students, such as strike the center two plates, then raise the mallets up to simulate a rest (BORDUN, REST), or hit the middle plates followed by the outer plates (contrary motion, which involves two sides of the body moving in a sequence away and toward the midline). These two patterns would be the next in order of difficulty in a progression from simple to complex.

Students number the four lined-up plates 1–4 from left to right. Other mallet patterns (progressing from easy to more difficult) that they might lead are these:

- Plates 1 and 2 followed by plates 3 and 4, or plates 1 and 3 followed by plates 2 and 4, or vice versa

- Plates 1 and 2 followed by right mallet alone on plate 4, or plates 3 and 4 followed by left mallet alone on plate 1

- Alternating crossover patterns: 1, 2, 4, 2, or 4, 3, 1, 3

Facilitation and Reflection

What motions were the easiest (hardest) to do with the mallets on the plates?

How did you decide what tempo to use when you were the leader?

How would you describe the pattern you led?

Are there any other instruments on which we would see similar patterning, with or without mallets? (piano, organ, xylophone, bells)

Extensions

Students work in small groups to design a mallet accompaniment to *Popcorn* (RM7) or *Hadarim* (CD4).

While sitting, pat the legs and pat the floor on either side to simulate the patterns the mallets performed—an example of the **simplify** strategy.

While standing, jump or step the feet in the same patterns. In place of plates, use squares on the floor or some other objects that will not slide.

Use eight plates, and design patterns.

Key Experiences
in Movement
and Music

Moving in locomotor ways

Expressing creativity in movement

Moving in sequences to a common beat

Describing movement

Grade 1 and above

40 Creating Designs

Students create a design by planning a sequence of locomotor movements that will be used for their design. The completed design is drawn on paper before it is performed.

Materials

Paper and markers

Activity to Experience

Students, with a partner, design a floor pattern they will travel using locomotor movement.

Students decide on the locomotor movements they will use for their design and when each movement will change.

Students draw their design on a large sheet of paper and then try it out using the selected movements.

Any changes of movements are incorporated into the overall design, tried out, and then demonstrated for the class.

Facilitation and Reflection

As you think about creating your designs with locomotor movement, what locomotor movements might you use?

How will you decide when to change your movements? How will you create your design?

Describe your design.

When are floor patterns, which are like designs, used? (for dance, for sports, for marching formations)

Extensions

One partner performs a locomotor movement in a pattern on the floor, and the other partner draws the design created.

Yarn is used to construct a design using the three basic pathways (straight, curved, zigzag). Movements for each pathway are chosen, and the design is put into movement.

Use different vocal representations of the pathways to accompany each movement selected (music key experiences: *exploring the singing voice*).

Also see Activity 35.

Curriculum
Concepts

Representation

Creativity

Responding to music

Key Experiences
in Movement
and Music

Moving with objects

Expressing creativity in movement

Describing movement

Moving to music

Grade 1 and above

41 Creative Paper Plates

Students work with a paper plate held in each hand, responding to the music with movement, first in personal space and then in general space.

Materials

Recording of an instrumental selection, such as *Hole in the Wall* (RM4), *Mîndrele* (CD5), or *Argós Hasápikos* (CD5).

Activity to Experience

Students listen to part of the recording, then discuss how the music makes them feel and what kinds of movement might represent that feeling.

Students explore various nonlocomotor (anchored movement) responses to the music in personal space.

Students explore moving in general space to the music while continuing to work with the plates at various levels and in various directions.

Students work as partners or in small groups to interact with one another using the plates.

Partners or groups may wish to share some of their movements with the class.

Facilitation and Reflection

How would you describe the mood of the music?

What types of movements did you like to perform to this music?

Describe one of the movements you chose.

When you worked with a partner or group, how did you keep from touching one another with the plates?

How does this type of creative movement differ from movement we have choreographed for folk dance?

Extensions

Students may wish to create a movement score to sections of the music, which they then perform.

Working with a partner, students can join paper plates by holding their two plates back-to-back and then move with the plates united.

Use the plates for mirroring and for reversal movements. See Activities 47 and 70.

With the backs of the plates taped to the palms of the hands, draw pictures in the air.

Use the plates for aerobics. See Activity 51.

Key Experiences
in Movement
and Music

Moving in locomotor ways

Describing movement

Expressing creativity in movement

Grade 1 and above

42 Estimating Distance and Time

Students estimate how many specific locomotor movements or how much time it will take them to reach a partner who is standing a specified distance away.

Materials

Watches or stop watch

Foot rulers and yardsticks

Activity to Experience

Students explore making even-sized loco-motor movements (walking steps, jumps, hops).

Working as partners, students decide what distance they will put between themselves and their partners. If space is limited, all partners may use the same distance, e.g., the distance across the classroom.

One student chooses a locomotor move-ment and estimates how many walking steps (jumps, hops) it will take to cover the distance to his or her partner. Then he walks (jumps, hops)

the distance to see how close the estimate is. The partner repeats the estimation process using the same or a different locomotor movement.

Students estimate and measure distance by using the feet heel-to-toe or by counting off lengths with other parts of their body. For example, they might "walk" the distance with a hand or a forearm to see how many hand or forearm placements it takes to cover a given distance. Students estimate the distance before using the movement.

Students also decide on the amount of time it will take to walk (jump, hop) a specified distance. Use a watch or stop watch to determine the time.

Facilitation and Reflection

How did you make your walking steps (hops, jumps) equal-sized?

How did you figure out how many of your walking steps (hops, jumps) it would take to cover the distance?

What can you do to come closer with your estimation the next time you try to estimate a distance?

How would you compare the locomotor movements for distance between movements? Which seem to cover the shortest distance? Which the longest distance?

How did you decide how much time it would take to cover the distance?

Extensions

Students can measure the distance (with a standard measuring instrument such as a ruler) after estimating and walking, hopping, or jumping the distance. Then they calculate in feet and inches the length of each walking step (jump, hop).

Students might decide to measure the length of their own feet in inches and estimate the number of steps (without knowing the exact measurement of the distance).

Estimate the number of walking steps (jumps, hops) that can be made in a specified time.

For younger children, see Activity 11.

Curriculum
Concepts

Spelling

Steady beat united with singing

Key Experiences
in Movement
and Music

Moving in nonlocomotor ways

Feeling and expressing steady beat

Singing alone and in groups

Grade 1 and above

43 Spelling Song

Students spell words while patting or rocking the macrobeat. They sing the song with the spelling.

Materials

Let's Sing a Song About a Word
(Bingo)

Traditional Tune

Let's **sing** a song a-**bout** a word and **this** is how it's **spelled,** oh.

H - o - u - s - e, h - o - u - s - e,

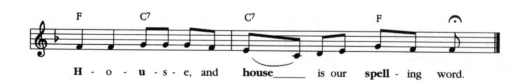

H - o - u - s - e, and **house**_____ is our **spell** - ing word.

Activity to Experience

Students decide on words they wish to spell. They rock and/or pat the steady beat and spell the words, using one, two, or three letters for each rock to make it fit the melody of the song. Examples with the rocking beat boldfaced are given in the diagram at right.

The teacher sings the song and inserts the spelling word. Students join in when they are ready. *Note:* If the word has three letters, the spelling part of the song is sung "**C**-a-**t** spells cat."

Students may decide they wish to step the beat. When the spelled word has an even number of letters, there is one step for each letter. When the spelled word has an uneven number of letters, some letters may be combined on each stepping beat, or there may be pauses in which no letter is sung. Adjust the spelling to fit the beat in the most natural way.

>		>	
X		X	
c	a	**t**	

>		>	
X		X	
h	o	**u-s**	e

>		>	
X		X	
f	u	**d**-g	e

Facilitation and Reflection

How did you think of the words differently when you were spelling them to a beat?

How did the song make it easier? Harder?

What other facts to be learned could you put into a song with a beat?

Extensions

Older students: Use longer spelling words, as shown at the right.

Use multiplication tables and other math operations.

The students can make up different words to the song. For the spelling part

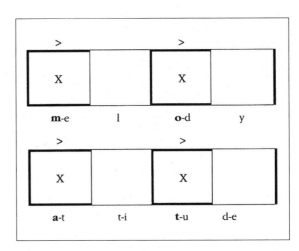

>		>	
X		X	
m-e	l	**o-d**	y

>		>	
X		X	
a-t	t-i	**t-u**	d-e

of the song, use a three-letter word and add a rhyming word, like this (rocking/patting beat is bold):

      C-a-t **rhymes** with hat,

      C-a-t **rhymes** with hat,

      C-a-t **rhymes** with hat, and

      Cat and hat are **rhym**-ing words.

See Activity 85, which uses the same melody in a similar activity with categories of nouns.

Grade 2 and Above

Key Experiences
in Movement
and Music

Moving in nonlocomotor ways

Acting upon movement directions

Describing movement

Grade 2 and above

44 From Back to Front

Students explore making and identifying geometric shapes and capital letters, "drawing" or "writing" them in the air and on each other's backs.

Materials

None

Activity to Experience

Students explore movement, "drawing" geometric shapes and letters in the air and on the floor with two hands joined and using nonlocomotor (anchored) movement.

Each student then "draws" a shape or letter on the back of a partner with two hands, first telling the partner whether it will be a shape or a letter. *Note:* Encourage students to at first use shapes and letters in which the fingers are kept in contact with the back while they are drawing.

The partner responds to the tactile communication, first paying attention to how the shape or letter is being drawn on his or her back, and then drawing it in the air with two hands joined, in front of himself or herself. The partner then changes roles.

Students may suggest that numbers or musical notes be drawn. They may also suggest that the person whose back is the drawing surface draw in the air simultaneously, while feeling the shape or letter on the back. *Note:* If the latter method is used, the person drawing should be encouraged to draw slowly. Remind students to continue to use two hands joined for drawing.

Facilitation and Reflection

Describe how you are making the geometric shape or letter. Where did you begin?

What did you do to figure out how the shape (letter) was drawn by your partner?

When drawing in the air while someone draws on your back, what helps you to have success?

Extensions

Reverse the roles. One person draws the shape or letter in the air, then the partner draws it on his or her back.

One person draws one line at a time with two fingers (using both hands) or one finger, and follows it with one to five taps on the back. It the line is drawn from low to high with two fingers simultaneously, followed by two taps, the partner does two jumps straight ahead. If one finger is used from high to low on the back, followed by three taps, the partner does three hops backwards. If the fingers alternate on opposite sides of the back, a walking movement is indicated.

For an additional tactile activity, see Activity 30.

Key Experiences
in Movement
and Music

Describing movement

Moving in locomotor ways

Acting upon movement directions

Grade 2 and above

45 Hearing and Responding

Students, working as partners, give each other verbal directions for ways to travel about the space. The partner responding to the verbal directions is blindfolded or has eyes closed.

Materials

None, or blindfolds for half of the students

Activity to Experience

Each student takes a partner. The partners practice giving each other verbal directions (without demonstrating) for locomotor movements, such as "jump forward four times." The signal to stop can be given by the leader at any time to avoid collisions with others.

One student in each pair puts on a blindfold or closes eyes and follows the verbal directions of the partner. All the students are moving about the space at the same time. The signal to stop is given by the leader when needed to avoid collisions.

The activity continues, with the other partner blindfolded.

Facilitation and Reflection

To the person blindfolded: What types of directions were easiest for you to follow? Hardest?

To the person giving directions: How did you decide what locomotor movements to give your blindfolded partner so no collisions occurred?

When might you need to give someone verbal directions for movement without being able to show them what to do? (giving directions to the driver of a car, helping a pedestrian or a bike rider to avoid a collision)

Extensions

Rather than working with partners, younger students can individually give verbal directions to the entire class.

The blindfolded partner may be asked to repeat the directions before acting upon the verbal directions.

The students may decide to give multiple directions before the partner responds.

Students, with their partners, can work across the gym using only forward and backward directions—a **simplify** strategy. Sideward directions can be added for movement across the gym. (The student would face one of the ends of the gym for this response.)

Locomotor movement extensions (size, level, intensity) can be added, as well as movement combinations (two jumps and one hop).

This same activity may be used with nonlocomotor movement.

Curriculum
Concepts

Mirroring

Visual tracking

Key Experiences
in Movement
and Music

Acting upon movement directions

Moving with objects

Moving in nonlocomotor ways

Grade 2 and above

46 Mirroring

Students hold a paper plate in each hand. After exploring slow dynamic movements they can do with the plates, they take a partner and visually lead the partner, who mirrors the movements. Music is added.

Materials

Two paper plates for each student

Recording of slow music, such as *The Sally Gardens* (RM1), *Tsamikos* (CD2), or *Southwind* (RM1).

Activity to Experience

Students explore slow dynamic movements with the paper plates, first without music and then to the musical selection *The Sally Gardens* (RM1). Encourage students to try symmetrical movement with both hands (or arms) and movement with one hand or the other hand.

Students, working in pairs, each face a partner and lead him or her with slow dynamic movements, which the partners visually mirror by watching and copying.

After both partners have had a chance to be the leader, students respond to the musical selection and lead their partners.

Individual students volunteer to be the leader for the entire class.

Facilitation and Reflection

As your partner moved, which movements were the easiest to mirror? Which ones were the hardest to mirror?

What strategies did you use to follow your partner successfully?

How did your movements change when the music was added?

When might you have to watch and copy someone who is using dynamic movement? (learning sport skills, learning to play instruments, trying to do what brother or sister is doing)

Extensions

Partners place their paper plates so they touch. They move the plates together, with one partner designated to initiate the movement.

Perform patterns of leg movements, and integrate moving the legs with the arm movements while holding plates.

Choreograph a sequence of movements to perform to the music.

Substitute other objects, such as scarves or rhythm wands.

Grade 3 and above: Partners try right and left reversal. See Activity 70.

Pre-grade 2: Partners copy without thought of mirroring or reversal.

Key Experiences
in Movement
and Music

Acting upon movement directions

Describing movement

Moving in nonlocomotor ways

Grade 2 and above

47 Moves to Remember

A leader molds a partner into a statue shape. The partner describes each movement after it is finished and remembers the order of the movements. After "erasing" the statue, the partner forms it again, using the same sequence of movements from memory.

Materials

None, or blindfolds for half of the students

Activity to Experience

Each student in the class has a partner. One student in each pair is blindfolded. The leader begins to mold the blindfolded partner into a statue shape. After each single movement, the statue describes the movement ("You placed my right arm over my head with the elbow bent").

In the next part of the activity, each pair of students works toward performing a sequence of movements from memory. The partner who is the statue decides how many movements he or she wishes to remember, do, and describe as a sequence. The leader continues molding the statue as before, guiding movements one at a time that the statue describes at each step. As they do this, both students make an effort to remember the sequence. *Note:* The teacher may wish to limit the total number of movements used to four and then raise the number to whatever the class suggests.

In the last part of the activity, the pairs carry out their movement sequence from memory. The partner who is the statue first thinks about the order of the movements, then "erases" the statue, and then forms the statue again, using the same movements in the same order.

If the statue has any problems in remembering the sequence, the statue-maker prompts him or her by using hands-on guidance.

Facilitation and Reflection

To the blindfolded partners: What types of movements were easiest to describe? What helped you remember the order of the movements?

To the partner making the movement decisions: How did you decide what movement to do? How did you decide on the order of the movements? What helped you remember the sequence?

What other activities or events require us to remember a sequence? (plays in sports, sequences in a drama, order of adding ingredients when helping to make cookies)

Extensions

The leaders might try to form themselves into the statues they created for their partners, using the same order of movements.

The leader might first tell the statue about each movement before moving a particular body part into the desired position. This involves planning and describing. In this extension, the blindfolded partner (statue) does not describe the movement.

Number the moves in Spanish or French, or in the language a class member speaks at home.

Number the moves so the leader can request the statue to do the "third movement followed by the fourth movement," etc.

Echo movements also require students to remember movements. See Activities 25, 26, and 64.

Curriculum
Concepts

Sequencing

Combining moving and speaking

Key Experiences
in Movement
and Music

Describing movement

Feeling and expressing steady beat

Moving in sequences to a common be

Moving in nonlocomotor ways

Grade 2 and above

48 Moving to a Rhyme

Groups of students join four two-movement sequences together with learner SAY & DO and then add the eight movements to a known four-line rhyme.

Materials

None

Activity to Experience

Students explore two-movement sequences with learner SAY & DO.

Working in pairs, partners teach each other their two-movement sequences. They unite those two sequences into a four-movement sequence with learner SAY & DO.

Two sets of partners join, and each pair teaches their four-movement sequence to the other pair. They unite those sequences, with learner SAY & DO, into an eight-movement sequence.

When the total sequence is secure and has been repeated several times, the sequence is joined with a four-line rhyme, such as "Hickory, Dickory, Dock." Each line is synchronized with one of the two-movement sequences performed on the macrobeat.

Students may wish to perform the sequence on the microbeat. In this case, each two-movement sequence is repeated twice before adding the next two-movement sequence, or the complete sequence is performed twice to accompany saying the rhyme.

Facilitation and Reflection

How did you decide which sequence would be first in the four-movement sequence? In the eight-movement sequence?

In what other ways have we combined moving and speaking?

What other ways have we used sequences?

Extensions

Work with a longer or shorter movement sequence performed to a rhyme. For example, perform only one two-movement sequence throughout the rhyme.

Repeat the same four-movement sequence throughout the rhyme.

Grade 3 and above: While saying a rhyme, perform locomotor movements, as in Activity 13, or combinations of nonlocomotor and locomotor foot movements.

Grade 3 and above: Perform integrated movements to rhymes.

Curriculum
    Concepts

Sequencing

Steady beat

Space awareness

Musical phrase

Key Experiences
    in Movement
    and Music

Moving in locomotor ways

Moving with objects

Acting upon movement directions

Moving in sequences to a common be

Feeling and expressing steady beat

Moving to music

Grade 2 and above

49 Plate Dancing

Students stand on two paper plates and explore locomotor ways to move while keeping their feet on the plates. From the sequences that are shared, students create a dance to the music.

Materials

Two paper plates per person

Recording of a moderately slow instrumental selection, such as *Apat Apat* (RM4), *Tipsy* (RM6), or *Sun Flower Slow Drag* (RM9)

Activity to Experience

Each student places a paper plate under each foot. The students listen to the music and explore moving about the space. Ways to move are shared and copied by the class.

Students listen to and explore moving to the music with sequences of upper-body movement. Students volunteer to share their sequences, and the class copies.

In small groups, students design an eight-beat dance to the musical phrases. They share their creations.

A class dance is created and performed.

Facilitation and Reflection

In what ways did the music tell you a way to move?

How did you decide on the sequences to use in the dance? What other objects could be used for dancing?

Extensions

Create partner dances to the music.

Younger students travel with skating steps alone and then in short trains of two, three, or four people. Add music for the skating movement.

Do square dancing with paper plates under the feet.

Use paper plates for aerobic sequences. See Activity 51. For creative movement, see Activity 41.

Key Experiences
in Movement
and Music

Moving with objects

Moving in sequences to a common be[

Describing movement

Feeling and expressing steady beat

Grade 2 and above

50 Passing Game Lead-Up

Students synchronize their timing to pass an object back and forth to a partner and then around a circle.

Materials

One beanbag or some other object for each student to pass

Activity to Experience

Partners sit facing each other and pass a beanbag back and forth. To "pass" it, they place it on the floor in front of their partner while simultaneously saying the word "PASS." The partner then picks it up and "passes" it back with the word "PASS."

Partners pass two beanbags between them, synchronizing placing the bag on the floor with saying the word "PASS." To make it more successful, they add another word as they each pick up the beanbag, such as "WAIT." This added word while picking up the beanbag makes the passing into a two-beat ("PASS, WAIT") sequence.

When students are ready for the challenge, they form one large circle or two or three smaller circles. Each student has a beanbag. As a beginning **simplify** strategy, all the students can simulate passing their bags in one direction by saying "PASS" as they each place a hand in front of the person to the right (or left). They bring the hand back to simulate picking up the bag that has been passed to them, using some other word ("WAIT") with that motion.

Students incorporate the beanbag while retaining the learner SAY & DO (two motions synchronized to the two words). A rhyme, song, or recorded music may be added as skill becomes evident.

Facilitation and Reflection

When we were in the circle, what strategies helped everyone to pass at the same time?

What other sequences might we use to pass an object?

Extensions

See Activity 66.

Pass a ball by tossing it back and forth to a partner, and then add larger groups. For more complexity, give each person a ball, and all pass at once around a circle.

Curriculum
Concepts

Sequencing

Microbeat

Visual tracking

Musical phrase

Key Experiences
in Movement
and Music

Moving with objects

Moving in sequences to a common bea[t]

Feeling and expressing steady beat

Moving to music

Grade 2 and above

51 Plate Aerobics

Students hold two paper plates and explore ways to hit the plates together, to hit their body with the plates, and to sequence movements with the plates.

Materials

Two paper plates per person

Recording of an instrumental selection, such as *Mexican Mixer* (RM3), *Ziguenerpolka* (RM2), or *Tzadik Katamar* (CD2)

Activity to Experience

With one plate held in each hand, students explore ways to hit the plates against their body and then hit them together away from their body, such as overhead, to one side, under one leg, behind their back. They share their ideas.

Working as partners, students explore ways to create two-motion sequences with the plates. Partners share with the class.

Students listen to the music and explore movements that will go with the phrases and the sections of the music.

Students lead the class to the music.

Facilitation and Reflection

How did you hit the plates?

What sequences of movements were successful in this faster microbeat tempo? Were any movements changed when music was added?

What other objects might be used for fitness movements?

Extensions

Divide students into three groups, for the A, B, and C sections of the music: One group choreographs the A section movements; one group, the B section movements; and one group, the C section movements. The final piece is performed. The *Mexican Mixer* selection is organized as follows: AA (64 beats), B (64 beats), A (32 beats), C (64 beats), A (32 beats). *Zigeunerpolka* is A, B, C (16 beats each).

To **simplify,** use macrobeat, use all single movements, and omit the sequences.

Add leg sequences to the arm patterns, such as raising one knee up and hitting the knee, then hitting the plates together as that leg comes down and the foot steps.

Use the paper plates creatively as in Activity 41.

Curriculum
Concepts

Responding to visual cues

Thinking and language

Space awareness—direction

Key Experiences
in Movement
and Music

Moving in locomotor ways

Acting upon movement directions

Describing movement

Feeling and expressing steady beat

Moving to music

Grade 2 and above

52 Robots

Students are divided into partners. One partner is the robot, and the other partner gives hand signals for the desired movement direction. Music is added.

Materials

Recording of an instrumental selection, such as *Popcorn* (RM7) or *Kulsko Horo* (CD5)

Activity to Experience

Students explore robot-type movements and describe the types of movements they have chosen to use.

Students listen to the recording of *Popcorn* and synchronize their movements to the beat of the recording.

Students individually decide on the hand signals they will use to direct their partner's movements *toward* and *away, to one side* or *to the other side,* and to *stop.*

Students work as partners, directing each other's movements with the hand signals that the partners have agreed upon.

Partners extend the experience by moving to the beat of the music when they are ready to do so.

Facilitation and Reflection

Describe how your legs moved like a robot.

What made your partner's hand signals easy or difficult to follow?

What are some other times when you might watch and follow someone's hand signals? (policeman, sign language)

Extensions

Verbal directions are given to the robots. Refer to Activity 45 for an example of giving verbal directions.

Robots synchronize steps and motions and create a robot dance.

Tactile signals are given to the partner. (For example, two taps on the outside of the right shoulder means to move two steps to the right side.) An additional tactile experience is found in Activity 47.

Use sign language to give movement directions in a visual way.

Key Experiences
in Movement
and Music

Moving in nonlocomotor ways

Moving in sequences to a common bea

Feeling and expressing steady beat

Acting upon movement directions

Describing movement

Moving to music

Grade 2 and above

53 Same and Different

Working as partners, students lead each other in movement to which the response is either the same or different but always in the same timing the leader is using.

Materials

Recording of an instrumental selection, such as *Bechatzar Harabbi* (RM6) or *Bekendorfer Quadrille* (RM4)

Activity to Experience

Students listen to the recording and explore nonlocomotor (anchored) movements to the beat of the music. Several volunteers share their movements to the music, and all copy.

Pairs are formed, the leader in each pair shares one of the movements he or she explored, and the follower copies. (Music is not used with this step.) The follower tries to perform the movement with the same timing used by the leader. *Note:* A successful strategy for the follower is to SAY a word that corresponds to the leader's movement before copying the movement. For example, the follower might say "SWING, SWING, SWING, SWING" before joining the movement.

Leaders demonstrate their nonlocomotor movements again, and the followers try to do a different type of movement but use the same timing that the leader is using. (Leader may be swinging the arms; follower may choose bending and straightening.) *Note:* Again suggest that followers SAY the word corresponding to the movement they will use before beginning.

Leaders match their movements to the beat of the music, and followers copy with the same movements and then with different movements.

Facilitation and Reflection

What nonlocomotor movements did you feel fit the music?

What did you find to be helpful when you were trying to copy the leader? What did you call your partner's movement?

What do we mean when we say we use "the *same* movement"? When we say we use "a *different* movement"?

Can you think of other times when you might copy the movement of a leader (do the same movement) or create a movement different from that of a leader?

Extensions

Younger learners: One person may wish to lead the class.

For a **simplify** strategy, omit the synchronization of movement to music.

Students may decide to use all single or all sequenced movements.

The concept of *same* movement could be used with extensions: A leader swings arms back and forth in front of the body. The follower swings back and forth but in a different direction or at a different level or intensity.

Curriculum Concepts

Steady beat

Making sounds

Identifying sounds

Key Experiences in Movement and Music

Moving with objects

Acting upon movement directions

Feeling and expressing steady beat

Describing movement

Exploring and identifying sounds

Grade 2 and above

54 Sounds

Students explore sounds they can make with their sticks. They also create sounds that keep steady beat.

Materials

Bobbins (8-inch quills) or rhythm sticks

Activity to Experience

Students explore making sounds by hitting the bobbins together or against their bodies. Individuals share their explorations with the class.

After several students have shared how they made their sounds, they explore how to keep steady beat with the sounds. Individuals share and then add words that label the sounds or movements, thus creating learner SAY & DO. (The words are added after the class successfully copies.)

Facilitation and Reflection

What does your sound remind you of?

What types of sounds with movement were easiest (hardest) to follow?

What types of movements with the bobbins were easiest (hardest) to perform in steady beat?

What sounds might you hear during the day that are in steady beat?

Extensions

Walk a steady beat while using the bobbins in a rhythm pattern.

Extend single steady beat movements to sequences of steady beat movements, such as two taps of the large ends of the bobbins, one rub of the metal, and one hit of the bobbins together.

Use other objects for beat, such as paper plates and unpitched percussion instruments (wood block, triangle, drum). See Activity 51.

Use the bobbins as mallets to strike paper plates turned upside down. This provides a preparatory exploration before the barred instruments are used. See Activity 39.

Younger students (grade 2 or under) can keep steady beat and create simple beat patterns, such as one tap on the knees, then one tap on the shoulders.

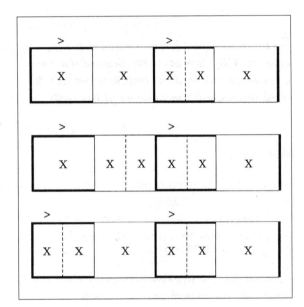

Record steady beat sounds heard during the day, and represent them with movement.

Grade 3 and above: With the bobbins, create four-beat rhythm patterns like the ones shown here. In these beat-box diagrams, each "X" represents a movement with the bobbins.

Kinesthetic awareness of movement

Thinking and language

Steady beat

Moving in locomotor ways

Describing movement

Expressing creativity in movement

Feeling and expressing steady beat

Moving to music

Grade 2 and above

55 What Else Do You See?

Students listen to the music, explore locomotor movement, and decide on a specific movement they wish to perform to this musical selection. Before showing the movement, a student leader decides on one aspect of the movement to describe. Followers add information about other aspects of the movement.

Materials

Recording of an instrumental selection, such as *Apat Apat* (RM4), *Twelfth Street Rag* (RM5), or *Jambo* (RM7).

Activity to Experience

Students listen to the recording, explore various locomotor responses, and decide on a locomotor movement they will share.

Each student determines one aspect of the movement that he or she will verbally share with others. For example, the student can say, "Each step will move from heel to toe."

In groups of three, one leads the others with the chosen movement. No music is playing.

When all stop, each follower shares an additional aspect of the movement performed, e.g., "The steps were large," or "The arms swung out to the sides in big movements."

The other students take their turns as leaders of their groups.

The followers recall all the movements, performing them without their respective leaders.

The music is played, and each leader in turn leads to the music.

Facilitation and Reflection

Describe the movement you chose to represent the music.

What was there about the music that made you want to move in the way you did?

How did you decide what to first tell your group about your movement?

Extensions

With younger learners, you may wish to have one person at a time lead the entire class.

Play another musical selection, explore movement to it, and discuss how the movement changed for the second musical selection.

Students may write about the movement they led and how it fit the music.

Grade 3 and Above

Curriculum
Concepts

Coordination

Sequencing

Tracking an object

Key Experiences
in Movement
and Music

Moving with objects

Moving in sequences to a common beat

Moving to music

Grade 3 and above

56 Flipping Sticks

Each student works with a stick held in each hand. Students explore ways to tap parts of their body with the ends of the sticks, to flip the sticks, and to pass the sticks from hand to hand. Then they develop sequences.

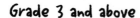

Materials

One pair of lummi sticks per person (or PVC pipe cut in 10"–12" lengths as a substitute)

Optional: Instrumental selection from *Rhythmically Moving* or *Changing Directions*, such as *Bechatzar Harabbi* (RM6), *The Hustle* (RM9), or *Erev Ba* (CD1)

Activity to Experience

Students explore tapping parts of their body and hitting the sticks together.

Students are encouraged to try half flips with the sticks, beginning with one hand and then the other hand alone, followed by two-handed flips. Students are reminded that learner SAY & DO (saying "FLIP" as the sticks are caught) aids success. Sequences are suggested by the students or the teacher and performed to a common beat. A sequence might include one flip and three rests, or two taps and a flip. Try adding known songs to the sequences.

Students explore changing the sticks from one hand to the other by tossing both sticks simultaneously. This new way of manipulating the sticks is added to the sequences.

Students may suggest choreographing sequences to recorded music.

Facilitation and Reflection

What helped you be successful when you flipped the sticks? When you passed them?

When we added the song, was there anything that helped you do the sequences while singing?

What was the easiest (hardest) movement you tried with the sticks?

Are there other times when you have to track (follow) the motion of an object?

Why is tracking someone else's motion harder than tracking your own?

Extensions

Partners may wish to work together and pass the sticks back and forth as in lummi stick games.

Students may suggest creating a whole-group choreography with the sticks.

Sounds may be added (music key experience: *exploring and identifying sounds*)

Younger students may wish to copy one another's movements with the sticks, as in the picture above. See Activity 36.

Curriculum Concepts

Understanding *greater than* (>), *less than* (<) symbols and numbers

Representation

Key Experiences in Movement and Music

Describing movement

Moving in nonlocomotor ways

Acting upon movement directions

Grade 3 and above

57 Greater or Lesser Numbers

Students work with the symbols < and >, using nonlocomotor movement. They use movement to represent the answers to the problems, using learner SAY & DO with their number.

Materials

Cards, each with one of the numbers 4 through 8 written on it

A card with the *less than* (<) symbol

A card with the *greater than* (>) symbol

Activity to Experience

Students explore with their bodies the *greater than* (>) and *less than* (<) symbols and share their ideas with the class.

Students each draw a number from 4 to 8 and represent the drawn number by using nonlocomotor movement with learner SAY & DO. (For example, if 4 was drawn, the student swings both arms 4 times saying "SWING, SWING, SWING, SWING.")

One student shows the card with the symbol for *greater than*. The others then each represent with locomotor movement a number that is greater than the drawn number, using learner SAY & DO. For example, if Jacob has drawn the number 4, and the leader presents a > symbol, Jacob could say "6 is greater than 4," and then proceed to use SAY & DO with a nonlocomotor movement (swing) 6 times. He might say "SWING, SWING, SWING, SWING, SWING, SWING" in time to his movements.

Once the students understand the activity, they may continue in partners or small groups so that more students have the opportunity to be the leader.

Facilitation and Reflection

What are some ways to show with your body the symbols for *greater than* and *less than*?

How did you remember what symbol the leader was showing on the card?

How did you plan your solution with learner SAY & DO so you knew when you reached the final movement?

What other ways do you see the *less than*, *greater than* symbols used? (accent mark, getting louder and getting softer, as the end of an arrow, acute angles)

Extensions

The leader shows his or her number and then, with learner SAY & DO, represents a number less than or greater than that number. The class indicates whether the number demonstrated was less than or greater than the leader's number. Then each person represents the same number as the leader, using a different movement.

Repeat the activity using locomotor movement or movement with objects. The class might choose ball bounces or taps of the rhythm sticks for the movement.

Form groups of one less than (<) or one greater than (>) a given number when the appropriate symbol is shown. Groups choose a movement and synchronize it, using learner SAY & DO.

Sounds may be added (music key experience: *exploring and identifying sounds*)

Curriculum
Concepts

Representation

Understanding positions of
numerals on clock face

Telling time

Key Experiences
in Movement
and Music

Moving in locomotor ways

Acting upon movement directions

Grade 3 and above

58 Human Clock

Students, working with imaginary clocks, move to the numerals on the edge of those imaginary clocks. They also use the two legs in movement to represent specific times selected.

Materials

Card with a clock face drawn on it

Activity to Experience

Groups of students review how the face of a clock has numerals around its outer edge.

Students stand in the center of their own imaginary clock faces and explore moving with locomotor movements from the center of their clock face to specified numerals on the outer edge of the face, as shown on the drawing on the opposite page.

Students, in small groups, give one another problems to solve with movement, such as, "You are facing 12. Jump to 3." *Note:* In the beginning it is easier to use a common starting place, returning to face 12 in the center of the clock after each problem. (See drawing.)

Students may decide to represent a specific time, such as 10 minutes after 6:00. They represent it by moving the two feet to the numerals 2 and 6 in the way the leader indicated they move, such as jump or hop to one number (6) and step to the other (2). Groups may wish to pose similar problems to the rest of the class.

Facilitation and Reflection

When Jason gave the problem of jumping to the numeral 5 and then to the numeral 7, how did you solve that problem?

When Alicia gave the problem of representing 10 minutes to 4, how did you solve that problem? (Students could jump from the center and land both feet simultaneously on the two numerals, or they could place one foot at a time. If the latter, ask which foot was placed first.)

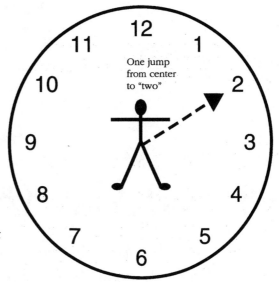

One jump from center to "two"

When we travel around the room in a dance sequence and we use the words "clockwise" and "counterclockwise," what do we mean?

What other things have a face similar to a clock face? (compass, dials on the stove, score clocks, stop watches, etc.) Are they numbered the same way?

Extensions

The arms can point in the direction of the two numerals for the time given.

A certain number of steps can be taken to the first numeral for the time; retrace those steps to return to the center, and then move to the second numeral.

Grade 4 and above: The points of a compass may be used instead of the numbers on a clock face. Now the students begin by facing north and move to the east, south, northwest, and so on.

Curriculum
Concepts

Thinking and language

Aural responding

Planning

Body and space awareness

Key Experiences
in Movement
and Music

Acting upon movement directions

Describing movement

Moving in nonlocomotor ways

Grade 3 and above

59 Matching Statues

Two students in each group of four stand facing away from each other and each of these two students forms a statue shape. The other two students, alternately giving one verbal direction at a time to each of the statues, try to make the statues match.

Materials

None

Activity to Experience

Groups are formed consisting of four students each. Two of the students in each group face opposite directions, so they can't see each other, and each makes a statue shape.

The other two students in the group each give verbal directions to one of the two statues, trying to describe how he or she can copy the partner's statue.

One of the direction-givers begins by giving a single verbal direction to the chosen statue, who then acts upon the verbal direction. The other direction-giver then gives a single verbal direction, to which the other statue responds. The object is to eventually have the two statues match with no visual cues being given. *Note:* The statues should not be directed to create a position that is totally different from the original statues (such as directing one statue to "stand up" and then directing the other statue to "stand up"). This would not follow the intent of creating a match between the statue shapes. Repeat the activity with the partners who were statues now becoming the direction-givers.

Facilitation and Reflection

To the statues: What types of directions were easiest for you to respond to?

To the persons giving verbal directions: How did you decide what direction to give your statue first?

What strategies did you use to make the statues match?

Extensions

In a second-grade class, create team A and team B. Two students are selected (one from each team) to form statue A and statue B. With a screen between them, the two statues face the class. The two teams alternate giving directions to their statues (Team A to Statue A and Team B to Statue B). The goal is to have Statue A match Statue B.

Simple statue-matching can be used with younger students. Students can copy the statue made by one person in the class or work as partners and copy each other. See Activity 19. See also Activity 24, which is an extension of Activity 19.

Key Experiences
in Movement
and Music

Moving in locomotor ways

Acting upon movement directions

Describing movement

Grade 3 and above

60 The Sum Moves Like this

Students work alone or with partners to represent two numbers with two different locomotor movements. The class gives the sum of the two numbers. The leader indicates the action to be used with learner SAY & DO, so all perform the designated movement the number of times needed to represent the answer.

Materials

None

Activity to Experience

Students select two numbers and decide on two different locomotor movements to represent the respective numbers. *Note:* You may wish to limit the sum of the two numbers to 12 or less.

A pair of students uses movement to present the two numbers to the class. Example: Jane jumps 4 times and then Mike steps 6 times.

The class gives the sum of the two numbers. Jane and Mike have indicated the class should skip their answer, so they skip 10 times, moving about the space. As they skip, they use learner SAY & DO, matching the skipping action to the word "SKIP" spoken 10 times.

A different pair of students presents the next pair of numbers to be added.

Facilitation and Reflection

How did you decide what movements to use to represent your numbers?

What strategies did you use to figure out the sum?

How did you keep track of the number of times you performed the locomotor movement when you were using learner SAY & DO?

Extensions

The leader represents one number (addend) and a sum. The class decides what other number is needed to arrive at the given sum.

The leader gives only the sum, and partners show two numbers that add to that sum.

Give subtraction problems using the same strategies.

Give three-step problems—two additions plus one subtraction.

Partners write the problems on paper after each solution is determined.

Use nonlocomotor movement instead of locomotor movement.

Curriculum
Concepts

Integrating movements

Musical form

Key Experiences
in Movement
and Music

Moving in integrated ways

Moving in sequences to a common bea

Feeling and expressing steady beat

Moving to music

Labeling form

Grade 3 and above

61 Aerobic Integration

Students unite arm and leg patterns to produce an aerobic fitness routine.

Materials

Recording of an instrumental selection, such as *Jessie Polka* (RM8) or *Irish Washerwoman* (RM3)

Activity to Experience

Students working in small groups explore lower-body locomotor and nonlocomotor sequences they can use for an aerobic routine and then explore upper-body nonlocomotor sequences.

Students work on integrating arms and legs in aerobic sequences. Different groups' ideas are shared with the class and tried out.

Students listen to the music and decide on sequences that seem to best fit the music. They work with the form of the music (AABB). *Note:* Because this is an aerobic routine, the microbeat is used throughout.

Students devise an aerobic routine that they feel is most appropriate for the music. They lead their routine for the rest of the class to follow.

Facilitation and Reflection

What movement sequences did you feel successful using?

When you integrated the movement sequences, what seemed to be the most successful arm and leg movement combination?

When can we use integrated sequences of movement other than in aerobic routines?

Extensions

One student might wish to lead the class extemporaneously to the music.

Try other musical selections, and compare the movements chosen for different tempos.

Younger students can lead nonlocomotor or locomotor movements with or without music.

Choreograph an aerobic routine to the music.

Use the integrated movements with a low platform (step aerobics).

Use objects, such as paper plates. See Activity 51.

Key Experiences
in Movement
and Music

Describing movement

Moving in sequences to a common bea

Moving in integrated ways

Feeling and expressing steady beat

Grade 3 and above

62 Combining Beat and Rhythm

*Students layer rhythmic sequences in the upper body against four
steady walking beats. Working in groups of four, students create
longer movement pieces of 16-beat duration.*

Materials

None

Activity to Experience

Students create sequences of arm movements
in a four-beat rhythm pattern decided on by
the class. They use learner SAY & DO in performing the sequences. The rhythm might be
the one shown at right.

The arm movements are CLAP for the first beat, PAT both knees at once for the second
beat, SNAP/SNAP with alternating hands on the third beat, and PUSH both arms away
from the body on the fourth beat.

Students try their sequences while walking to the steady beat.

Students are encouraged to share their sequences, and all copy.

Students decide to work with partners. They create other sequences of movement to different four-beat rhythm patterns. They walk steady beat while performing the sequences.

Students select groups of four and choreograph a 16-beat movement piece by combining
each person's 4-beat rhythmic sequence.

Facilitation and Reflection

What movements in the rhythm pattern did you find easy to sequence? Difficult to sequence?

What strategies did you use to keep the underlying beat steady?

How did you decide on the order of your 16-beat rhythm pattern?

How many different ways can we define rhythm?

In what other ways might we experience rhythm?

Extensions

Choreograph hand-jives with partners. See Activity 65.

Perform the movement sequences to music.

Begin with single movements, such as all pats or all snaps, in the rhythm patterns (alternate the hands).

Keep the steady beat in the upper body and walk rhythm patterns. See Activity 73.

Key Experiences
in Movement
and Music

Describing movement

Feeling and expressing steady beat

Moving in nonlocomotor ways

Moving in sequences to a common bea

Labeling form

Grade 3 and above

63 Combining Sequences

Students construct four-movement sequences. Partners teach their sequences to each other with learner SAY & DO. They decide on which sequence will come first as they unite their sequences into an eight-movement sequence.

Materials

Recording of *Bekendorfer Quadrille* (RM4)

Activity to Experience

The music is played, and each student selects a four-movement sequence to perform to the macrobeat.

Each student joins a partner, and the partners teach their four-movement sequences to each other with learner SAY & DO. They unite their sequences into an eight-movement sequence. They SAY the sequence and then SAY & DO.

Students will enjoy the challenge of two pairs joining to make groups of four. All teach their sequences, which are united with learner SAY & DO, to form a 16-movement sequence.

Each person leads to the music—first person to the A sections, second, third, and fourth persons to the B, C, and D sections. (Each repeated section of the music has 16 macrobeats. Thus a person's sequence is led four times in succession.)

The second time the music is played they may decide to unite the first and second persons on the A (eight movements), the third and fourth persons on the B (eight movements), and then all four on the 16-movement sequence performed to the combined C and D sections of the music.

Facilitation and Reflection

What teaching strategies did you use for your sequence?

How did you decide on the order of the sequences?

What are some other occasions when we might have long sequences of movements?

Extensions

On the third repeat of the four sections of the music, have someone randomly call out the order of the sequence, such as third person's, second person's, first person's, fourth person's. Or, have first and fourth persons unite their sequences followed by the second and third.

Try performing a canon movement sequence. This means that the second person begins on the B section of the music but with the first person's sequence, etc. If the first person begins on the A section of the music with arms doing OUT, IN, UP, DOWN and then doing HEAD, SHOULDERS, KNEES, SHOULDERS for the B section, the second person begins with OUT, IN, UP, DOWN as the B section of the music begins.

Perform the eight movements in reverse, beginning with the last movement and ending with the first movement.

Can two groups join for a 32-motion sequence? If students suggest it, the challenge is worth the time to try it.

See Activity 68.

Key Experiences
in Movement
and Music

Moving in nonlocomotor ways

Feeling and expressing steady beat

Moving in sequences to a common bea

Moving to music

Grade 3 and above

64 Echo Canon

Students review single and sequenced nonlocomotor movements using steady beat. They lead one another in canon movement without music and then synchronize their movements to music.

Materials

Recording of *Hot Pretzels* (RM8) or *The Hustle* (RM9); optional, for extension: *Oh, How Lovely* (RM1)

Activity to Experience

Students review and explore their own single and sequenced nonlocomotor movement, keeping steady beat for the movement. The movements are performed at a slow tempo.

Students recall the concept of *canon*. The teacher leads the class in canon movement, beginning by performing two slow single movements. The followers begin with the teacher's first two movements as the teacher continues with the second two movements. The class is watching the new movement while performing the one completed by the leader. The followers start at the beginning while the leader goes on, so the followers are always behind in copying the movements of the leader, as shown in the beat-box diagram, opposite page. This procedure reinforces the musical concept of *canon*.

Students in small groups work with canon movement, beginning with all single movements. After each student has had the opportunity to lead, the groups may decide to try two-beat sequenced movements. Each sequence would be shown two times before it is copied. The leader proceeds to the new sequence while the followers do the completed one.

Leader:							
X	X	X	X	X	X	X	X
pat	pat	snap	snap	clap	clap	push	push

Followers:							
		X	X	X	X	X	X
		pat	pat	snap	snap	clap	clap

Play the music for students to work with in macrobeat. When leading, they begin the two-macrobeat movement at the start of the musical phrase.

Facilitation and Reflection

What does the concept *canon* mean?

As we perform movement that will be followed with the *canon* concept, what strategies can we use to remember the movement to copy and prepare for the new movement to copy?

When you are the leader, how do you hold your concentration and prepare for the next movement, beginning it at the right time?

When might you see the idea of a *canon* used? (singing, orchestra pieces, a person signing as someone is speaking)

Extensions

Begin with single movement and sequenced movement echo. See Activities 25 and 26.

Divide into groups of three, and plan echo canon movements to the music *Oh, How Lovely* (RM1). (There are six macrobeats in each of the three sections of the music.)

Echo after a four-movement sequence, so the copying begins after eight microbeats of music.

Key Experiences
in Movement
and Music

Moving in nonlocomotor ways

Moving in locomotor ways

Feeling and expressing steady beat

Moving in sequences to a common beat

Moving to music

Grade 3 and above

65 Hand-Jives

*With a partner, students choreograph sequences of movement to the
steady beat, first without music and then to the musical phrases.*

Materials

Recording of a musical selection, such as *Mexican Mixer* (RM3), *Salty Dog Rag* (RM9),
or *Sneaky Snake* (RM4); optional, for extension: musical selection in ABC form, such as
Zigeunerpolka (RM2)

Activity to Experience

Students, working with partners, explore body and hand-jive movements. These movements are combinations of hand or foot sequences performed alone and with a partner.
Encourage the use of learner SAY & DO. It will help students remember the sequence.

Here is an example of an eight-beat sequence:

 a. Clap your own hands.

 b. Hit palms together with your partner.

 c. Hit the outside of one foot with the corresponding hand while hopping on the
    other foot.

 d. Repeat with the other foot and hand.

 e. Clap your own hands again.

 f. Hit right palms together.

 g. Hit left palms together.

 h. Make a motion in front of your body with both thumbs up.

Students listen to the music, determine the beginnings and endings of phrases, and decide on an eight-microbeat movement sequence to perform to the eight-beat phrases of the music.

Students share their hand-jive sequences with the class. They may wish to decide on the order of their presentations, to keep the music playing. The first pair performs the sequence twice, followed by the second pair, etc.

Facilitation and Reflection

Recall the order of the movements you used. Which ones were performed without contact with your partner and which ones involved contact with your partner?

What strategies did you use to construct your sequence?

Can you think of other types of movement sequences you might perform alone or with a partner? (sports movements, dance, sign language)

Extensions

Two sets of partners might wish to work together. One pair plans the movements for the first section of the music, and the other pair plans movements for the second section. They teach each other their movements.

Try a circle hand-jive with the whole class or with a small group. Standing in a circle, students perform the movements decided on by the class or group. Each student performs movements alone and with the students standing to either side. For example, a girl might clap her hands, then hit the hands of the students on each side of her, and then pat the knee of the students on each side of her.

Try a foot-jive.

Work with other music in a different form, such as *Zigeunerpolka* (RM2) in ABC form.

Curriculum
Concepts

Passing

Sequencing

Steady beat

Key Experiences
in Movement
and Music

Moving with objects

Feeling and expressing steady beat

Moving in sequences to a common beat*

Describing movement

Grade 3 and above

66 Hand-to-Hand Passing

Students synchronize their timing to pass objects from one person's hand to another person's hand.

Materials

Beanbags or other objects—one per person

Activity to Experience

Students already have had experience with passing an object in Activity 50. They now are ready for the challenge of passing an object from hand to hand.

Students are seated in a circle and decide on which direction they will pass their beanbags around the circle (for example, to the right).

Everyone's left hand rests on the left leg, palm up. *The right hand becomes the passing hand.* Beginning with the right hand on top of the left, as the word "PASS" is spoken each person practices passing by moving the right hand to the left hand of the person who is sitting to the right. Each person returns the right hand to the starting position as a word, such as "RETURN," is said.

Beanbags are held in the left hand. All simultaneously take the beanbag with the right hand and move it as practiced. Using learner SAY & DO keeps the timing synchronized.

The group reverses the process, passing the beanbag to the left.

Facilitation and Reflection

What strategies did you use to try to stay together so all the beanbags were passed at the same time?

In what other ways might we use the concepts of *passing* and *sequencing*?

Extensions

Students may suggest putting other movements into the sequence, such as tossing and catching: "PASS, HOLD, TOSS, CATCH." Now the receiving hand must move to the leg as the passing hand passes the beanbag.

Use Activity 50 to synchronize passing in a simpler way.

Students standing in a line pass balls over their head or between their legs. Every other student has a ball. Add learner SAY & DO.

In small groups, students pass balls by each person tossing his or hers to the next person. Each student has a ball.

Curriculum
Concepts

Integrating movement

Visual tracking

Layering movement for integration

Key Experiences
in Movement
and Music

Moving in integrated ways

Acting upon movement directions

Describing movement

Grade 3 and above

67 Integrated Movement Copycat

Students work in pairs, with each student leading integrated movements for a partner to copy. One partner begins with a leg pattern and layers on an arm pattern. The student who is the follower recalls and describes the pattern.

Materials

None

Activity to Experience

Students explore sequenced foot patterns and then layer arm patterns onto them. Several students share their movements with the class.

Students form pairs. Half of the class, with their partners, are on one side of the gym, and half are on the other side.

Partners on one side of the gym go first. The leaders begin their locomotor leg patterns, which the followers copy. Leaders then layer on the arm pattern, and the followers copy.

When the first set of partners reaches the opposite side of the gym, the followers describe the movements to their leaders by recalling the patterns.

The partners in the other half of the class take their turns and repeat the process.

Facilitation and Reflection

How did you decide what arm sequence to add to the leg pattern?

What helped you copy your partner's movements?

What helped you remember the leg and arm patterns so you could recall them?

What are other occasions when we see integrated movements used (sport skills, marching band)?

Extensions

Copy integrated movements that are not layered.

Try the strategy of layering with several of the sports skills.

Leaders might wish to synchronize their movements to music. Use integrated movement sequences. See Activity 68.

Curriculum
Concepts

Sequencing

Integrating movements

Key Experiences
in Movement
and Music

Moving in integrated ways

Moving in sequences to a common beat

Feeling and expressing steady beat

Moving to music

Labeling form

Grade 3 and above

68 Integrated Sequences

Students design two integrated movements to fit the two-part musical selection.

Materials

Recording of a two-part (AB) instrumental selection, such as *Sauerländer Quadrille* (CD3) or *La Bastringue* (CD2)

Activity to Experience

Students recall integrated movement sequences they have used before and explore new ones.

Students listen to the two-part music, identifying where the parts begin and end.

Students are guided to plan two different integrated movements to fit the two sections of the music. Examples they might use are jumping jacks or make-believe jump-rope (turning an imaginary rope). The A and B sections of the music have 32 beats each and are played three times.

Facilitation and Reflection

What integrated movements have we experienced?

Was there anything about the music that guided you in choosing what movements to use?

How did you decide the order to use for the two movements?

Extensions

Use objects, such as paper plates or balls, with the integrated movements.

Do all the movements in place or travel on some of them.

Keep the arm or leg movements the same and change the opposite ones. This would be a **simplify** strategy.

Use integrated aerobic movements.

See Activity 63.

Curriculum
Concepts

Visual tracking

Space awareness—direction

Reversing an image

Key Experiences
in Movement
and Music

Moving in locomotor ways

Moving in integrated ways

Acting upon movement directions

Moving in sequences to a common beat

Grade 3 and above

69 The Moving Circle

Students are standing in a circle. A student leader, inside the circle, performs locomotor movements without speaking, and the class follows the movements in the same direction (e.g., leader moves clockwise, followers move clockwise). Another leader adds an arm movement.

Materials

None

Activity to Experience

Students plan and explore movements in different directions—in and out, sideward, forward, backward in space.

One student volunteers to be the leader and begins a movement sequence consisting of IN, IN, IN, KICK; OUT, OUT, OUT, TOUCH. The class copies the movement in the same timing as the leader. (See drawing to right.)

Another student uses SIDE, CLOSE in a clockwise direction, which all copy. (See drawing, next page.) This student adds a SNAP, CLAP integrated with the foot pattern.

The activity continues with other student leaders deciding on sequences of movement for the class to process and respond to.

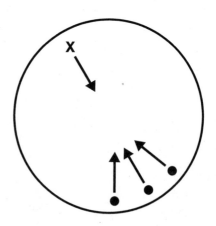

Leader and followers: IN, IN, IN, KICK

Facilitation and Reflection

Why did you choose that hand pattern to go with the foot pattern?

What helped you decide how to move and what direction to follow if you faced the leader from across the circle?

What strategies did you use to respond accurately to the movements when the leader demonstrated moving arms and legs at the same time?

What are some other times when you need to respond to movement directions?

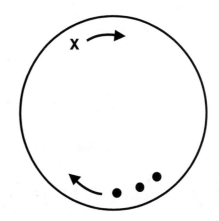

Leader and followers: SIDE, CLOSE, SIDE, CLOSE

Extensions

Students follow nonlocomotor sequences.

Students perform aerobic sequences together to music.

Students use the same side of the body the leader is using (e.g., leader uses right, students use right).

See Activity 70, next.

Curriculum Concepts

Image reversal

Visual tracking

Key Experiences in Movement and Music

Moving in nonlocomotor ways

Acting upon movement directions

Grade 3 and above

70 Reverse That Image

Using the same side of the body as they face the leader, students copy single static movements (they copy right side with right side, left side with left side). Slow dynamic movements are substituted as the students gain experience in reversal.

Materials

None

Activity to Experience

Students, working in small groups, explore and discuss movements that would be easier or harder to copy accurately when facing the movement leader. (They are using the same side—right hand copies right hand; thus it looks "reversed.")

One student volunteers to face and lead each group (or the entire class) with single static movements that the followers copy not by mirroring but by *reversing* the image (i.e., using *their* right when the leader uses *his* or *her* right).

Once the followers are successful at reversing static movements, the leader can face the group and demonstrate slow dynamic movements at a tempo that permits students to use reversal in copying the movements.

Facilitation and Reflection

What movements did your group decide would be easy to follow? Hard to follow?

What strategies did you use to reverse the movement image correctly?

What do we have to do to successfully follow visually when the leader does not pause between movements?

When in class have you been expected to use the same side as the leader when the leader is facing you? (standing across the circle when the teacher was showing dance steps, fingering the recorder)

Extensions

Integrate arms and legs for the students to mirror, or reverse. Again begin with static movements before slow dynamic and with ipsilateral (same arm and leg) before contra-lateral (opposite arm and leg) movements.

Use objects held in the hands.

Lead movements to music.

See also Activity 69.

Key Experiences
in Movement
and Music

Moving in integrated ways

Feeling and expressing steady beat

Labeling form

Moving to music

Grade 3 and above

71 What Beat Shall We Use?

Students, in groups of three, decide on three different ways to express beat to the A, B, and C sections of the music.

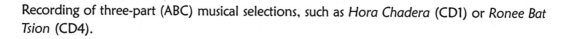

Materials

Recording of three-part (ABC) musical selections, such as *Hora Chadera* (CD1) or *Ronee Bat Tsion* (CD4).

Activity to Experience

The recording is played, and students explore walking to the microbeat and macrobeat. They also explore keeping macrobeat and microbeat with movements in the upper body.

Students in groups of three discuss and then explore combinations of nonlocomotor and locomotor movements, using macrobeat and microbeat. Students share with their group.

Students decide which movements to use during each of the three sections of the music. The upper and lower body can both represent the macrobeat or microbeat, or one part of the body can represent one beat while the other part represents the other beat.

Facilitation and Reflection

Which beat did you explore first with your feet? Why? Which beat did you explore first with your arms? Why?

Describe how you put together your arm and foot movements.

When might someone need to represent both the microbeat and macrobeat at the same time? (aerobics, dance)

Extensions

Use sequenced movements to the music.

Move one area of the body at a time in either macrobeat or microbeat for each section of the music.

Choose other three-part music.

Younger students: Play the "beat detective" game in Activity 29.

Curriculum
Concepts

Integrating movement by
learning parts

Sequencing

Musical form—AB

Key Experiences
in Movement
and Music

Moving in integrated ways

Moving in sequences to a common bea

Feeling and expressing steady beat

Labeling form

Moving to music

Grade 3 and above

72 Adding Arms to the Dance

*Students choreograph a dance and design arm sequences for each
section of the dance.*

Materials

Recording of musical selection in AB form, such as *Yankee Doodle* (RM2) or *Bannielou
Lambaol* (RM8); optional, for extension: *Limbo Rock* (RM2) or *Pata Pata* (RM6)

Activity to Experience

Working in small groups, students choreograph a dance to the AB form of *Yankee Doodle*.
They work on the foot patterns first.

Then the task for each group is to create arm sequences that can be integrated with the
foot patterns.

Each group shares their integrated movement, and the class tries out the sequences.

A class choreography is constructed from the ideas presented.

Facilitation and Reflection

How did you decide what foot patterns you would use in each of the two sections of the
dance?

How did you decide what arm sequences would fit with the foot patterns?

Describe how the arms and legs fit together in the sequence you developed. ("When we stepped to the side, the arms went to the side.")

What are some tips to remember when you try to follow an integrated pattern?

How did you represent the AB form of the music?

Extensions

Create integrated movements for other American novelty selections, such as *Limbo Rock* (RM2) or *Pata Pata* (RM6).

Learn the arm sequences for folk dances.

Experience other integrated movement in Activities 61 and 67.

Curriculum
Concepts

Three and four-beat conducting
patterns

Steady beat

Sequence

Key Experiences
in Movement
and Music

Moving in integrated ways

Feeling and expressing steady beat

Moving in sequences to a common bea⸱

Moving to music

Feeling and identifying meter

Grade 3 and above

73 Conducting and Walking

Students integrate the three- and four-beat conducting patterns with a variety of walking sequences.

Materials

Recording of *Likrat Shabat* (CD1), *Le'Or Chiyuchech* (RM8), or *Tsamikos* (CD2)

Activity to Experience

Students listen to the music and try out various four-beat walking sequences, such as "WALK, REST, WALK, REST" or "WALK, WALK, WALK, REST."

Students recall the four-beat conducting pattern (shown at right), using both arms. They SAY & DO the pattern "DOWN, IN, OUT, UP" and then repeat this pattern to the music.

Students practice integrating the walking sequences with the learner SAY & DO of the arms. They try out a number of different sequences.

Students decide on the walking sequences the class will use with the recording. All perform to the music.

Four-beat conducting pattern

Right hand is shown with unbroken line.
Left hand is shown with broken line.
Learner SAY & DO is the same for both hands.

Facilitation and Reflection

What walking sequences were the easiest (hardest) to perform to the music while conducting? Why?

Where in the pattern did you find the rests hardest to perform? Why do you think it was hard to put the rests there?

What other examples of integrated movement can you think of that would be more successful if you used learner SAY & DO with the arm pattern?

Extensions

Hold paper plates or short sticks for the conducting pattern.

Try a three-beat conducting pattern (shown at right) integrated with foot patterns. The learner SAY & DO is "DOWN, OUT, UP."

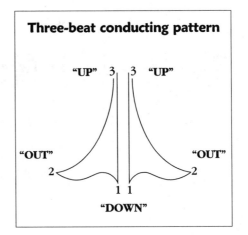

Three-beat conducting pattern

Key Experiences
in Movement
and Music

Moving in locomotor ways

Feeling and expressing steady beat

Moving to music

Grade 3 and above

74 Grand March

Students work together to decide on routes they might travel around the room as they march in single file, march with a partner, or march in lines of four or eight persons.

Materials

Recording of *Jessie Polka* (RM8) or other instrumental selections from the *Rhythmically Moving* or *Changing Directions* recordings or the *Rhythmically Walking* cassette tape (*Rhythmically Walking* is preferred, if available)

Activity to Experience

Students explore various pathways that all can use as they march in the gym or around the classroom. They decide on a single-file route to travel.

In the gym, students explore pathways and formations that can be used in traveling single file, with a partner, or in fours or eights. They plan their route. An example is the following section of a grand march: moving down the center by twos, then separating into two single-file lines at the end of the gym, with each line going to the corner and then turning and going up the outside and then marching diagonally across the room to meet again as twos in the center of the gym, as shown at left.

The twos could also alternate in turning opposite directions at the end of the room, coming around and joining to go back down the center of the gym by fours. A spiral can be wound and then unwound.

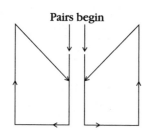

Pairs begin

Pairs of students may decide to face each other and slide sideward down the center, or they may skip or gallop side-by-side down the center. The ideas to be generated are unlimited.

Facilitation and Reflection

What are some of the pathways you took in the gym (classroom)?

When might you see this type of marching outside of school?

Extensions

Parades or trains of approximately two to four students may move about the space.

Students may make a map of their route.

Make up a sequence of locomotor movements for a grand march using AABB music. The sequence could be as follows. A section: March eight steps, jump four times, and hop four times; then repeat the A section. B section: Skip eight times, tiptoe four steps, and accent feet (heavy steps) four times; then repeat the B section.

Use the sequence above for canon movement. Half of the class begins. The other half of the class begins the A section when the first group begins the B section.

Curriculum
Concepts

Acute, obtuse, and right angles

Key Experiences
in Movement
and Music

Moving in nonlocomotor ways

Acting upon movement directions

Describing movement

Grade 3 and above

75 Identifying Angles

Students use nonlocomotor movement to explore right angles, acute angles, and obtuse angles. Two students in each group of three students create statue shapes that are joined. The third person identifies and labels all the angles found in the statue shapes.

Materials

None

Activity to Experience

The class divides into groups with three students in each group. Groups review acute, obtuse, and right angles and then explore the angles they can make with their body.

Two students in each group form statue shapes that are attached to each other in some way. The third student in the group finds and identifies the angles created by the joint statue.

The activity continues, with the other two students taking a turn at identifying the angles created by the statues.

Facilitation and Reflection

How would you describe each of the angles—right, acute, and obtuse?

In the statue shapes, where did you find right angles? Acute angles? Obtuse angles?

As you look about the room, where do you find these angles?

Extensions

A problem-solving task could be given to create as many right angles as possible in one- or two-person statues.

The third person may wish to guide the formation of the two-person statue, one angle at a time, identifying the angle formed with each move.

The student leader may wish to draw an angle on a card and have the class respond with locomotor movement to travel a pathway that forms that angle.

A volunteer may draw one card from three prepared cards showing the three kinds of angles. The volunteer identifies the kind of angle and demonstrates a way to use movement to represent it, and all copy.

Use yarn to represent the angles and travel the yarn shape using locomotor movement.

Curriculum
Concepts

Representation

Vocal exploration

Key Experiences
in Movement
and Music

Moving in nonlocomotor ways

Moving in locomotor ways

Expressing creativity in movement

Exploring and identifying sounds

Grade 3 and above

76 Machines That Work

Students work in groups of six to eight. Each group selects a machine or form of transportation and constructs a working representation of that machine. Representative vocal sounds are added to the movement. Each group shares, and the class guesses what is being represented.

Materials

None

Activity to Experience

Students form groups of six to eight. Groups brainstorm to list machines or forms of transportation they might represent with movement and sound. When each group has decided what to represent, they tell the teacher what they have chosen, so two groups don't select the same machine.

Students plan and carry out how they will represent their machine with nonlocomotor or locomotor movements and what vocal sounds will accompany the movements.

Groups volunteer to share their representations with the class, so the class can guess what is being represented.

Facilitation and Reflection

What did you consider first as you selected the machine or form of transportation you would represent?

How did you decide what movements to use? What vocal sounds to use?

What else could you represent with movement and sound?

Extensions

Kindergarten students might represent the different forms of transportation they know about.

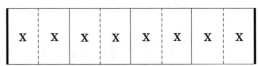

Older students might demonstrate science concepts: levers, or molecules, or sound waves.

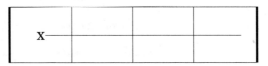

Represent the machine with steady beat movements using the following durations within the same machine.

Key Experiences
in Movement
and Music

Moving in locomotor ways

Describing movement

Moving in sequences to a common be

Expressing creativity in movement

Grade 3 and above

77 Shaping Sequences

Students choose one of four geometric shapes and represent the shape with sequenced locomotor movements. Each student joins another student with a different shape, and they join their sequences. Each student finds three other students, and they construct an eight-movement sequence.

Materials

Sets of four geometric-shape cutouts (one cutout for each student)

Activity to Experience

Each student selects one of the four geometric shapes and represents that shape with a sequence of two different locomotor movements or the same locomotor movement performed twice in two different positions. All perform each sequence with learner SAY & DO. Examples might be the sequence "JUMP, HOP," or a sequence "SIDE, CLOSE," or "APART, TOGETHER" with two jumps.

Each student takes a partner who has a different shape. They teach each other their sequences using learner SAY & DO and then put the two sequences together into a four-movement sequence.

Each student finds three other students with three other shapes. After teaching one another their sequences, they determine the order of the four sequences, placing the shapes in that order. They may change a sequence if they determine it to be necessary to create an effective eight-movement sequence.

Facilitation and Reflection

Describe the sequence you created to represent your shape.

When you joined the second person, how did you decide whose sequence should come first?

How did you decide on the order of sequences for the eight-movement sequence?

If you changed any of the sequences, why did you feel you needed to make the change?

Are there occasions when people create long sequences of any type of movement? (Writing is a movement sequence, as are sports and dance skills.)

Extensions

With younger learners, begin with a single movement (nonlocomotor or locomotor) representing a shape. See Activity 22.

Select a dance step to represent a shape, such as cherkessiya, grapevine, schottische, two-step, etc., and sequence those dance steps together.

Substitute colors, sounds of instruments, or other objects to represent with movement.

Curriculum
Concepts

Directionality of movement

Straight and curved pathways (for writing and art)

Linear and rotary

Key Experiences in Movement and Music

Acting upon movement directions

Describing movement

Expressing creativity in movement

Grade 3 and above

78 Is the Movement Straight or Circular?

Students explore ways that nonlocomotor and locomotor movements can be performed in straight and curved (circular) pathways. Movements are demonstrated, copied, and described. These concepts are then related to an understanding of linear and rotary movement.

Materials

None

Optional, suggestions for extension: *Bannielou Lambaol* (RM8), *Dučec* (RM8), *Nebesko Kolo* (RM9), *Rumunjsko Kolo* (CD4)

Activity to Experience

Students review the concept of *directionality* of movement *(forward, backward, upward, downward, around)*.

In pairs, students explore ways that nonlocomotor and locomotor movements can be performed in straight pathways and in curved or circular pathways. Students demonstrate movements to the class; one pair volunteers to lead the movements and the rest of the students copy and describe the leaders' movements.

Students discuss the concepts of *linear motion* and *rotary motion*. They now combine linear motion with change of locomotor pathway—changing the movement with the change of direction.

They then work with rotary and locomotor movement, exploring ways to vary their movements. For example, they could explore small and large circular pathways, or change the direction of their rotary movements as they change their locomotor movements.

Facilitation and Reflection

What can we say about pathways?

How are straight and curved writing/drawing motions used during the day?

What movements were easiest in straight pathways? In curved (circular) pathways?

How do we apply linear and circular motions to drawing shapes or objects in art? In printing the alphabet? In writing numbers? In cursive writing?

Extensions

Younger children: See Activities 7, 28, and 35.

Show the linear and curved (circular) motions with yarn or other media.

Do the movements to AB music, changing the movements on the B section. Examples of AB music are: *Bannielou Lambaol* (RM8), *Dučec* (RM8), *Nebesko Kolo* (RM9), *Rumunjsko Kolo* (CD4)

Curriculum
Concepts

Synonyms and antonyms
Opposites
Same and different

Key Experiences
in Movement
and Music

Acting upon movement directions
Describing movement
Moving in sequences to a common beat
Feeling and expressing steady beat

Grade 3 and above

79 Synonyms and Antonyms

*Students review the concepts of **synonyms** and **antonyms** and explore their relationship to movement. Students volunteer to lead the group. Others in the class copy, describe, and give synonyms for the movement. They also choose and demonstrate a movement antonym.*

Materials

None

Activity to Experience

Students talk about the concepts of *synonyms* and *antonyms* and then explore ways to show the two concepts with movement.

As ideas are generated, several students volunteer to lead the class with their movements. Class members copy the leader, then talk about the word that describes the movement and some synonyms for it. They also try using a movement to demonstrate one of the synonyms. (Examples of synonyms: "punch," "push," "thrust," "press," "dab.") They talk a little more about antonyms and demonstrate a way to show an antonym for the leader's movement.

Other students demonstrate a sequenced movement, e.g., "bend and straighten." The class, after copying the movement, also gives other words that the movement could be called, e.g., "out/in," "far/near," "down/up."

Students list the synonyms and antonyms that were generated during the experience.

Facilitation and Reflection

What is the difference between a synonym and an antonym?

What examples of synonyms and antonyms did you choose?

What movements did you choose to show the concept of *synonym*? Of *antonym*?

Extensions

Perform the movements to recorded instrumental selections from *Rhythmically Moving* or *Changing Directions.*

Younger students: Use the concepts of *opposites* and of *same* and *different* with the movements demonstrated.

Begin with an action word, such as "shake." Try out synonyms appropriate to use with "shake"; then try out antonyms.

Curriculum Concepts

Triple meter

Tri—the prefix for three

Key Experiences in Movement and Music

Acting upon movement directions

Describing movement

Moving in sequences to a common bea[t]

Moving to music

Identifying meter

Feeling and expressing steady beat

Grade 3 and above

80 And Three It Will Be

Trios explore movement patterns in sets of three. They share their patterns with the class for others to copy and add SAY & DO. Patterns are performed to the music. Each trio makes a list of words that begin with "tri," meaning "three." These are shared with the class.

Materials

Recording in triple meter such as *Tsamikos* (CD2) or *D'Hammerschmiedsgsell'n* (RM7)

Activity to Experience

Each student joins two other students to form trios. They explore nonlocomotor movement patterns in sets of three. Directions are given to first try patterns in which beats 2 and 3 are the same movement (POUND, SHAKE, SHAKE). Then they try patterns in which all three beats are different (POUND, SHAKE, TAP).

Trios volunteer to share their patterns with the class for the others to copy. The copiers describe the pattern and decide on the SAY & DO to speak while performing the pattern. Several patterns are performed to the music.

Trios are given paper and pencil and instructed to make a list of all the words they can think of that begin with "tri" (meaning "three"), e.g., tricycle. The lists are shared with the class and a master list is created.

Facilitation and Reflection

What were the easiest patterns to perform? the hardest?

What do we mean by triple meter? How does it feel different from movement in *sets of two*?

What else could we do to demonstrate triple meter?

Extensions

Explore locomotor patterns in sets of three, beginning with patterns in which beats 2 and 3 are the same movement (e.g., JUMP, HOP, HOP).

Work with the triple jump, using HOP, STEP, JUMP.

Unite two sets of three movements into a longer pattern of six movements.

Conduct with both arms in groups of three (down, out, up) to *Tsamikos* (CD2) or *D'Hammerschmiedsgsell'n* (RM7). Learn the folk dances for these musical selections. See *Teaching Folk Dance: Successful Steps*, by Phyllis S. Weikart, for the dance directions.

Sing songs that have steady beats grouped in threes, such as "My Country 'Tis of Thee" and "Take Me Out to the Ball Game." Conduct with both arms or rock the macrobeat. (Music key experience: *singing alone and in groups*)

Curriculum
Concepts

Ratios

Steady beat relationships

Macrobeat and *microbeat*

Key Experiences
in Movement
and Music

Acting upon movement directions

Describing movement

Feeling and expressing steady beat

Grade 3 and above

81 Timing Relationships

Several students volunteer to lead nonlocomotor movement in a steady beat. The class copies in a 1 to 1 relationship (e.g., 1 pat to 1 beat). The teacher demonstrates a 2 to 1 relationship (2 pats to 1 beat) to a slower steady tempo.

Materials

None

Optional: Recording such as *Korobushka* (RM8), *Bulgarian Dance #1* (RM8), or *Danish Masquerade* (CD4)

Activity to Experience

Students move with steady beat using nonlocomotor movement. Several volunteer to lead, and the others copy movements in a 1 to 1 relationship (e.g., 1 tap to 1 beat). Students describe movement and the tempo.

The teacher copies a student's steady beat tempo with a 1 to 1 movement, then demonstrates a 2 to 1 relationship (patting the knees twice while stepping once) at a slower tempo. Class members join the teacher in the 2 to 1 movement and then do the same movement at the student leader's original, faster tempo.

All form groups of four and take turns leading and following in the 2 to 1 relationship. Followers rock back and forth to feel the beat relationship.

The teacher now copies a different, faster steady beat led by a student, alternating the hands in a 2 to 1 relationship. Class members join the teacher in alternating the hands in this faster tempo. They then return to two-handed movement, following the leaders's faster tempo and then the teacher's tempo. *Note:* Faster movements are always more accurate when sides of the body are alternated.

The groups of four now work with the 2 to 1 relationship in a faster tempo as they did with the teacher.

Followers try slower and faster 2 to 1 relationships, following the leader's tempo and then working with music. *(Korobushka* works well when a slower tempo and 2 to 1 relationship are needed. The first part of *Danish Masquerade* is a good selection for working with a 2 to 1 relationship at a slower tempo; the middle part may be used for the 3 to 1 relationship; and the third part, for the 2 to 1 relationship at a faster tempo.)

Facilitation and Reflection

What do we know about *macrobeat* and *microbeat?*

How would you define beat relationships?

How did we know that we were expressing a steady beat that was in a 2 to 1 relationship, even though the movements were sometimes slow and sometimes faster?

When might we want to understand and express a 2 to 1 relationship? (two glasses of milk, one twice as full as the other; two cookies for each child.)

Extensions

Work with relationships of 3 to 1, 4 to 1, or 5 to 1.

Use different musical selections with faster or slower tempos.

Use a stepping movement for 1 to 1 movement, and pat with two hands for the slower 2 to 1 relationship (feet and hands). Alternate the hands for the faster 2 to 1 relationship (hands to feet).

Travel with the feet in different tempos and express relationships of 2 to 1, 3 to 1, and so forth with the upper body.

Curriculum
Concepts

Addition, subtraction,
multiplication

Movement in sets of three

Key Experiences
in Movement
and Music

Acting upon movement directions

Describing movement

Moving in sequences to a common beat

Feeling and expressing steady beat

Grade 3 and above

82 Strengthening Math Facts

Students explore nonlocomotor movement in sets of three in which the second and third beats are the same movement. Volunteers share their movements and the class copies and describes them. SAY & DO is added (SHOULDERS, WAIST, WAIST).

Materials

None

Activity to Experience

Students are asked to explore nonlocomotor movement patterns in sets of three, with three movements followed immediately by the repeat of the movement pattern in steady beat. Volunteers share and all copy, followed by SAY and DO.

Then they explore a pattern in which the first movement is patting one place on the body and the second and third movements involve patting in a second place (knees, shoulders, shoulders). Volunteers share, and all copy, followed by SAY & DO with the body location names.

The teacher introduces SHOULDERS, WAIST, WAIST, which the students copy and label. These movements are repeated a minimum of four times.

The teacher introduces the math game and states the problem with the first two movements (3 + 3). There is silence with the third movement. Students echo the problem on the repeat of the movement pattern. On the next repeat, students say the problem with the answer on the third movement. This last step is performed four times. Then the teacher gives a new addition problem.

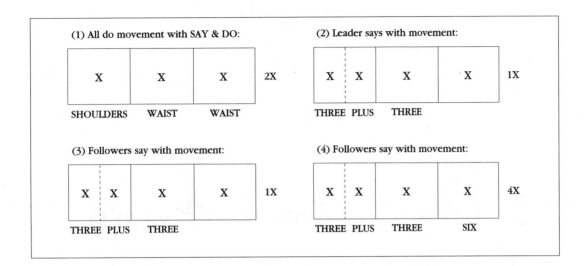

(1) All do movement with SAY & DO:

| X | X | X | 2X |

SHOULDERS WAIST WAIST

(2) Leader says with movement:

| X | X | X | X | 1X |

THREE PLUS THREE

(3) Followers say with movement:

| X | X | X | X | 1X |

THREE PLUS THREE

(4) Followers say with movement:

| X | X | X | X | 4X |

THREE PLUS THREE SIX

Facilitation and Reflection

What do we already know about movement in sets of three?

What helped you be successful?

In what other ways can we experience math facts with movement?

Extensions

Subtraction or multiplication problems can also be given.

Try the problems with three different movements, rather than with the second movement repeated (shoulders, waist, knees).

Sing the problem. The problem and class echo are sung with 5, 3, 3 (sol, mi, mi). The answer is given with 5, 3, 1 (sol, mi, do) (music experience: *developing melody*).

Curriculum
Concepts

Thinking in a forward order

Thinking backward to reverse a
given order

Key Experiences
in Movement
and Music

Moving in locomotor ways

Feeling and expressing steady beat

Acting upon movement directions

Describing movement

Grade 3 and above

83 Forward and Backward

Students try out walking forward then backward three steps followed by a rest. Three numbers, letters, or words are spoken in forward order (1, 2, 3, rest) followed by the same numbers, letters, or words in reverse (3, 2, 1, rest).

Materials

None

Activity to Experience

The teacher demonstrates by walking three steps forward followed by a rest and then three steps backward followed by a rest. The students are asked what they noticed. Students then try out the movement pattern.

The teacher gives a spoken direction, three numbers forward and then backward, then demonstrates how the words fit with walking forward and backward. Students try out the teacher's pattern several times.

Students plan a sequence of numbers, letters, or words. They try out the pattern with forward and backward movement in their own timing.

A student volunteers to be the leader, speaking the words for the forward movement; the others respond by saying the same sequence in reverse. Now everyone tries out the entire word pattern, adding the movement. The student leader speaks while walking forward, but the others do not speak with him or her. Then the others say the words in reverse as they travel backward. The group experiences each pattern a minimum of three times.

Facilitation and Reflection

Why was speaking information backward more difficult than speaking it forward?

What type of information was the most difficult for us to speak backward?

When might it be important to know how to reverse information? (when retracing one's path to find a lost object)

Extensions

Try the activity in pairs. One person plans the forward pattern and the partner responds in reverse.

Use locomotor movements, e.g., walking, jumping, hopping.

Speak a short line of a rhyme, e.g., "Peas Porridge Hot."

Curriculum
Concepts

Unequal patterns

Movement in groups of two
and three

Uncommon meter

Key Experiences
in Movement
and Music

Moving in locomotor ways

Moving in sequences to a common beat

Expressing creativity

Feeling and expressing steady beat

Grade 3 and above

84 Combining Groups of Two and Three

Students create unequal patterns, using two different locomotor movements, e.g., jumping and hopping. Students plan one of the movements to be done three times and the other two times. They SAY & DO.

Materials

None

Optional, suggestion for extension: *Lemonaki* (CD3)

Activity to Experience

The teacher tells the class that she is going to jump three times and then two times. She demonstrates three jumps using SAY & DO (JUMP, JUMP, JUMP) and two hops (HOP, HOP) She repeats the pattern, encouraging the students to join her and add SAY & DO.

Students now create their own patterns of locomotor movements in threes and twos. Several students share for all to copy.

A student leader suggests ways to create other groupings of two movements and then three movements. The teacher and the class respond to the student's suggestion.

Facilitation and Reflection

What other patterns might you see that have unequal groupings? (wallpaper border, design on floor tiles)

For older students: Why might it be important to try out these unequal groups of movement? (as a lead-up to understanding uncommon meter)

How did you remember how many movements you did using SAY & DO without counting?

Extensions

Use nonlocomotor movement first to create unequal groups. This makes the task simpler.

Do one movement lasting three beats and a second movement lasting two beats. In the example above, the jump would be the first of three beats and the hop the first of two beats. The pattern is JUMP, REST, REST, HOP, REST; JUMP, REST, REST, HOP, REST. Take out the word *rest* as soon as possible and feel the pause without labeling it.

Play a recording with a three-two-two beat pattern (1-2-3, 1-2, 1-2) such as *Lemonaki*. Match the first set of three beats (1-2-3) with one movement, and each of the two-beat sets with the second and third movements, completing the seven-beat pattern (three movements).

Curriculum
Concepts

Nouns and categories of nouns

Macrobeat

Musical form

Key Experiences
in Movement
and Music

Moving in nonlocomotor ways

Feeling and expressing steady beat

Moving in sequences to a common bea~

Labeling form

Singing alone or in groups

Grade 3 and above

85 Categories of Nouns

Students make lists of the three categories of nouns—person, place, and thing. They keep the beat with macrobeat movements during the song, then continue the movement and respond with a noun from the category chosen. Sequenced movements are added when students are ready.

Materials

Music below

Three Categories That Are Nouns

Text by Crystal Duncan
Catawba College, Salisbury, NC

Three ca - te - go - ries that are nouns, and ev - 'ry sen - tence has one.

Per - son, place, or thing; per - son, place, or thing;

per - son, place, or thing, and ev - 'ry sen - tence has one.

Activity to Experience

Students discuss what nouns are and make lists of nouns, arranging them under the three categories of *person*, *place*, or *thing*.

Students decide on one of the categories. One student begins a movement, setting a fairly slow tempo for the steady beat. All match the beat with the **anchor word** spoken by the leader. Students take turns saying a noun in the category. One beat occurs between each spoken word. For example, pat knees on the accented syllable of a noun spoken by one student, pat knees again before the next noun is spoken, pat knees with a second student speaking a noun. The following beat-box diagram shows how this would work for the category of place. Each "X" represents a pat. The accented syllables are in bold.

X	X	X	X	X	X	X	X

Boston		**Atlanta**		**Detroit**		**Dallas**	
first student		*second student*		*third student*		*fourth student*	

Students might work in groups of four or eight, so all students in the group have the opportunity to give a noun. Begin with single movements, and then later increase the complexity with two-motion sequences. The noun is spoken with the first movement.

Sing the song, keeping the macrobeat in the way the student leader chooses. At the end of the song, keep the beat and add the nouns for a total of eight macrobeats. Sing the song again, thus creating ABA form.

Facilitation and Reflection

What are several examples of nouns? Person nouns? Place nouns? Thing nouns?

How will you decide on the noun to use when it is your turn?

What can help us to keep the macrobeat steady?

What musical form did we use? Where else, other than in music, do you find the ABA form used? (Oreo cookie, pattern in a print)

Extensions

Give a noun on each macrobeat.

Sing the name of the noun, using pitches that are in the same key used for the song.

Walk macrobeat or microbeat while singing and giving the noun examples. If microbeat is used, students might choose to say the noun on the first of four walking beats, as shown below.

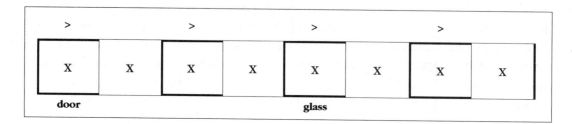

Another alternative is shown below. On the first macrobeat, one student says a noun on a rocking motion, and the group says the noun's category on the third macrobeat. (Macrobeats two and four are rocks without a noun or a category spoken.) The pattern continues as each student has a turn saying a noun and the group answers with a category.

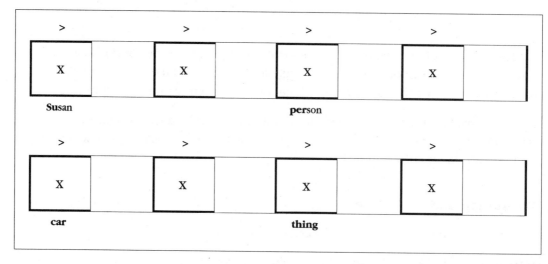

Glossary

active learning approach An educational perspective in which the teacher both introduces ideas and recognizes opportunities to support and extend ideas initiated by students.

alternating movement Movement in which two corresponding body parts take turns. For example, the two feet take turns in walking.

anchored Having some part of the body in fixed contact with the surface (floor or ground) while other body parts move.

anchor word (pitch) A single word spoken or sung by the leader four or eight times to bring the group to beat synchronization before saying a rhyme or singing a song. Singing this word on the beginning pitch of the song *(anchor pitch)* enables the group to begin with a common beat and pitch.

asymmetrical movement Movement in which two corresponding or two different body parts move at the same time in different ways.

aural The modality in which a learner listens, processes, and responds to spoken or sung directions.

basic timing Ability to independently feel and maintain the underlying steady beat of a rhyme, song, or recorded/live musical selection with nonlocomotor and locomotor movement. This ability is the intended outcome of the key experience *feeling and expressing steady beat.*

beat (steady beat) The consistent, repetitive pulse that lies within every rhyme, song, or musical selection. The pulse has even durations and occurs at equal intervals.

beat competence Demonstrated proficiency expressing and maintaining microbeat and/or macrobeat with nonlocomotor or locomotor movement while moving, singing, or playing instruments.

beat coordination Ability to perform sequences of movement to one's own steady beat and with others. This ability is the intended objective of the key experience *moving in sequences to a common beat.*

body awareness Understanding how each body part can move and what movement relationships exist among body parts.

choreography The art of creating and arranging sequences of movements to music.

cognitive Having to do with the process of mental learning or understanding.

concept An abstract idea fundamental to a specific body of knowledge.

contralateral movement Movement performed simultaneously by two different body parts on opposite sides of the body (for example, the right arm moving at the same time as the left leg).

creative movement Taking movement that is familiar and changing it in some way.

curl A nonlocomotor movement that involves motion at joints where there are short bones on either side, such as the spine, fingers, or toes.

direction An extension of movement that refers to "where" movement is going (upward/downward, forward/backward, sideward, around, clockwise/counterclockwise).

duple meter Meter based on groups of two beats or on multiples of two.

dynamic movement Movement that continues without pausing until the designated stopping point.

even timing Repeated movement having equal time intervals between the movements.

facilitate The third component of the Teaching Model. In this component, the teacher uses varied strategies involving action, thought, and language to engage learners and enable them to construct their own knowledge.

fine-motor movement Movements and coordinations of movements performed with small-muscle groups.

flow An extension of movement that concerns whether it is smooth or choppy.

form The organization or structure of a musical selection. For example, a selection can be in AB form, in AABB form, and so on.

gallop An uneven locomotor movement in which one foot is the leader and the other foot comes up to meet it.

general space All the available space within some large perimeter, such as the walls of a room or the boundaries of a playing field or court—all the space that a person can reach using locomotor movement.

gross-motor movement Movement (locomotor or nonlocomotor) of large-muscle groups.

hands-on-guidance Interacting with the learner by using the tactile/kinesthetic mode.

hop A locomotor movement that transfers weight from one foot to the same foot.

integrated movement Movement in which two different areas of the body are united in purposeful movement.

intensity An extension of movement that concerns how much force is applied.

jump A locomotor movement that transfers weight from one or two feet to two feet. The landing is on two feet.

key experiences Essential experiences that support the development of specific intended objectives that are relevant to a learner's understanding of a particular concept.

kinesthetic Pertaining to the processing and awareness of body movements.

language awareness An understanding of the labels associated with parts and actions of the body.

leap A locomotor movement that is a stylistic variation of running, involving greater height or distance.

learner SAY & DO The process whereby a learner chants a word and simultaneously performs a related movement, creating a cognitive-motor link.

level An extension of movement that shows whether the movement is in a low, middle, or high plane.

locomotor movement Nonanchored movement with transfers of weight in personal or general space.

macrobeat The rocking or patting beat that organizes groups of two or three microbeats. It coincides with the first beat of each group of two or three microbeats.

meter The grouping of beats in a pattern of two (ONE, two, ONE, two) or three (ONE, two, three, ONE, two, three) or combinations of twos and threes.

microbeat The regular walking beat; each beat of a group of two or three beats.

mirroring Copying a leader's movement, while facing the leader (follower's right arm copies leader's left arm).

nonanchored Having no part of the body in fixed contact with the floor, as in weight transfers.

nonlocomotor movement Anchored movement performed in one's own space (personal space) without complete transfers of weight.

note A musical symbol that denotes both pitch and duration.

one side ... other side Repeated movements of one arm, leg, or hand, without moving the opposite arm, leg, or hand. This is followed by doing the same repeated movements with the corresponding body part on the opposite side.

pathway An on-the-floor or in-the air pattern (straight, curved, zigzag) that the body creates with locomotor or nonlocomotor movement.

personal space All the space that any part of the body can reach while the body is anchored (when performing nonlocomotor movement).

phrase A musical (or spoken) thought that is part of a melody. One often stops to take a breath at the end of a phrase.

pull A nonlocomotor movement that applies a steady force toward the body.

push A nonlocomotor movement that applies steady force away from the body.

representation Movement that reenacts familiar actions or happenings or imitates various living things and creatures. It involves moving "like" or "as if."

reversal (right/left) Copying a leader's movement, while facing the leader, by moving the same side of the body the leader is using. For example, the follower's right arm copies the leader's right arm.

rhythm The duration of note values, words, or syllables within and among the beats of a rhyme, song, or musical selection.

rock A nonlocomotor movement that maintains the body in anchored position but partially shifts weight side-to-side or front-to-back.

SAY & DO *See* **learner SAY & DO.**

separate The first component of the Teaching Model; this component involves using only one mode of presentation—visual demonstration, spoken directions, or hands-on guidance—when presenting information to learners.

sequenced movement Two or more purposeful movements (such as bending and straightening) joined together; once it is completed, the sequence can repeat itself.

shape The appearance of a movement—whether it looks symmetrical, narrow, wide, curved, and so on.

simplify The second component of the Teaching Model, which means beginning with what is manageable for the learner. This may mean breaking a task into subtasks.

single movement One movement that is held or repeated (for example, patting knees, stomping one foot or stepping).

size An extension of movement that refers to whether it is large, medium, or small.

skip An uneven locomotor movement that is the combination of two different transfers of weight—gallop and hop. Skipping has uneven timing.

slide An uneven locomotor movement, which may be thought of as a sideward gallop.

space awareness Understanding the "where" and "how" of movement, the body's relationship to personal and general space.

static movement Movement that stops or pauses before a new movement is presented.

stretch A nonlocomotor movement in which force is exerted to extend the trunk, arm, or leg beyond the usual position.

swing A nonlocomotor movement that involves either forward-and-backward or side-to-side movement.

symmetrical movement Two (both) sides of the body doing the same movement at the same time.

Teaching Model A presentation method consisting of three components—**separate, simplify,** and **facilitate.** The Teaching Model is fundamental to the program's **active learning approach.**

tempo The speed of the song, rhyme, or musical selection.

time awareness The ability to understand whether a movement is fast/slow, even/uneven, and so on. All movement has timing.

tracking The act of visually following a movement.

triple meter Meter based on groupings of three beats or multiples of three.

turn A nonlocomotor movement that involves taking the arm, hand, finger, foot, or leg all the way around in a 360-degree movement; a locomotor movement that changes the facing direction.

two sides Corresponding body parts moving at the same time.

uneven timing When there are varied intervals of time between movements.

Alphabetical Index to the Activities

Kindergarten and Above

Activity		Page
8	Attributes of Shapes	.30
1	Creativity With Scarves	.16
2	Explore That Sound	.18
9	Listening and Identifying	.32
10	Lively Levels	.34
3	Low or High	.20
4	Musical Houses	.22
5	Names in Beat	.24
13	People in Our Town	.40
11	Planning to Step	.36
12	Seven Jumps	.38
16	Simon Says Variation	.46
6	Stop Sign	.26
7	Traveling Pathways Between Objects	.28
14	Understanding Spatial Concepts	.42
17	We Keep the Beat Together	.48
15	Who's Driving?	.44

Grade 1 and Above

Activity		Page
21	Action Words	.58
25	Beat Echo	.66
39	Beat-Keeping With Mallets	.94
23	Combining Words	.62
40	Creating Designs	.96
41	Creative Paper Plates	.98
22	Different Shape—Different Movement	.60
26	Echo Sequence	.68

42 Estimating Distance and Time 100
27 Extending Our Movements 70
38 How Many Points of Contact? 92
29 Is It Macrobeat or Microbeat? 74
18 Is the Pattern Even or Uneven? 52
28 Making Pathways in the Air 72
20 Matching Stick-Figure Poses 56
37 Numbers and Statue Shapes 90
30 Puppets 76
31 Pushing Up 78
32 Recalling the Past 80
43 Spelling Song 102
19 Statue Clones 54
24 Statues That Change 64
33 Stop and Balance 82
34 Trains 84
35 Traveling Pathways Without Objects 86
36 Who Matches Me? 88

Grade 2 and Above

Activity   **Page**
44 From Back to Front 106
45 Hearing and Responding 108
46 Mirroring 110
47 Moves to Remember 112
48 Moving to a Rhyme 114
50 Passing Game Lead-Up 118
51 Plate Aerobics 120
49 Plate Dancing 116
52 Robots 122
53 Same and Different 124
54 Sounds 126
55 What Else Do You See? 128

Grade 3 and Above

Activity   **Page**
80 And Three It will Be 180
72 Adding Arms to the Dance 164

61   Aerobic Integration 142
85   Categories of Nouns 190
62   Combining Beat and Rhythm 144
84   Combining Groups of Two and Three 188
63   Combining Sequences 146
73   Conducting and Walking 166
64   Echo Canon 148
56   Flipping Sticks 132
83   Forward and Backward 186
74   Grand March 168
57   Greater or Lesser Numbers 134
65   Hand-Jives 150
66   Hand-to-Hand Passing 152
58   Human Clock 136
75   Identifying Angles 170
67   Integrated Movement Copycat 154
68   Integrated Sequences 156
78   Is the Movement Straight or Circular? 176
76   Machines That Work 172
59   Matching Statues 138
69   The Moving Circle 158
70   Reverse That Image 160
77   Shaping Sequences 174
82   Strengthening Math Facts 184
79   Synonyms and Antonyms 178
60   The Sum Moves Like This 140
81   Timing Relationships 182
71   What Beat Shall We Use? 162

Musical Selections Provided With This Book

The following selections appear on the compact disk included with this book. Suggestions for appropriate activities are given for each selection.

1. *Apat-Apat* 49. Plate Dancing; 55. What Else Do You See?

2. *Bannielou Lambaol* 72. Adding Arms to the Dance; 78. Is the Movement Straight or Circular? 81. Timing Relationships

3. *Bechatzar Harabbi* 18. Is the Pattern Even or Uneven? 53. Same and Different; 56. Flipping Sticks

4. *Bekendorfer Quadrille* 53. Same and Different; 63. Combining Sequences; 71. What Beat Shall We Use?

5. *Cherkessiya* 19. Statue Clones; 36. Who Matches Me?

6. *Dučec* 31. Pushing Up; 78. Is the Movement Straight or Circular?

7. *Echo* 25. Echo; 26. Echo Sequence

8. *Gaelic Waltz* 1. Creativity With Scarves; 34. Trains

9. *Hole in the Wall* 14. Understanding Spatial Concepts; 41. Creative Paper Plates

10. *Hora Chadera* 4. Musical Houses; 29. Is It Microbeat or Macrobeat? 71. What Beat Shall We Use?

11. *Hot Pretzels* 4. Musical Houses; 64. Echo Canon

12. *Jessie Polka* 18. Is the Pattern Even or Uneven? 61. Aerobic Integration; 74. Grand March

13. *Korobushka*   15. Who's Driving? 34. Trains; 81. Timing Relationships

14. *La Raspa*   8. Attributes of Shapes; 33. Stop and Balance

15. *Likrat Shabat*   73. Conducting and Walking

16. *Mexican Mixer*   4. Musical Houses; 51. Plate Aerobics; 65. Hand-Jives

17. *Oh, How Lovely*   54. Echo Canon

18. *Peat Fire Flame*   8. Attributes of Shapes; 24. Statues That Change

19. *Popcorn*   39. Beat-Keeping With Mallets; 52. Robots

20. *The Sally Gardens*   46. Mirroring

21. *Sauerländer Quadrille*   22. Different Shape—Different Movement; 68. Integrated Sequences

22. *Seven Jumps*   12. Seven Jumps

23. *Tsamikos*   46. Mirroring; 73. Conducting and Walking; 80. And Three It Will Be

24. *Yankee Doodle*   18. Is the Pattern Even or Uneven? 29. Is It Macrobeat or Microbeat? 72. Adding Arms to the Dance

25. *Zigeunerpolka*   35. Traveling Pathways Without Objects; 51. Plate Aerobics; 65. Hand-Jives

About the Authors

Phyllis S. Weikart, Director of the Movement and Music Division, High/Scope Foundation, and developer of the program "Education Through Movement: Building the Foundation," is a nationally known and highly respected educator-author. She bases her writing on her ongoing work with students of all ages—preschoolers to senior citizens. Her other titles include *Teaching Movement & Dance* and *Round the Circle*.

Phyllis S. Weikart is Associate Professor Emeritus in the Division of Kinesiology, University of Michigan, and visiting Associate Professor at Hartt School of Music. Her formal education includes a B.S. degree from Arcadia University and an M.A. degree from the University of Michigan. In addition to being an educator and author of seven books, she is a researcher, curriculum developer, workshop leader, choreographer, and a producer of high-quality international folk dance albums (with 14 released albums). Her wide-ranging experiences have led to the development of a teaching approach that ensures teachers success with students of all ages.

Elizabeth B. Carlton is a Field Consultant for the Movement and Music Division, High/Scope Foundation. She brings to her writing many years of teaching experience with students of all ages. Having earned degrees in music performance and music education (BA, BME, MA) from Georgetown College, Kentucky, she has gone on to a varied career. An Assistant Professor Emeritus of Music at Catawba College, she is also a composer, curriculum developer, workshop leader, organist, piano teacher, and author (the primary author of *Foundations in Elementary Education: Music* and *Guides to Rhythmically Moving 1–5*).